The
real
life
mney
Journal

About the Author

When Clare Seal reached what seemed like a breaking point in her relationship with money in spring 2019, she turned to Instagram to make herself accountable, posting anonymously about her journey out of debt as @myfrugalyear. She immediately struck a chord, and in just one year found a following of 45k people, with her posts offering advice and solidarity to a growing community of people in a similar situation. This led to her first book, *Real Life Money*, in which she shared her story and provided her readers with honest, realistic guidance and support for how to understand their own relationships with money. A new voice on the finance scene, Clare has been sought out by the *Telegraph*, *Huffington Post*, *Grazia* and *Hello!* magazine to give her opinion on topics relating to debt, money and the challenges facing millennials. She is a working mother of two, and lives with her husband and children in south-west England.

The
real
life
m£ney
Journal

clare seal
@myfrugalyear

First published in 2020 by Headline Home
an imprint of Headline Publishing Group

1

Cataloguing in Publication Data is available from the British Library

ISBN 978 1 4722 7903 3

Commissioning Editor: Anna Steadman
Senior Editor: Kate Miles
Copy Editor: Tara O'Sullivan
Designed by Steve Leard
Proofreader: Nikki Sinclair

Printed and Bound in Europe by the GPS Group

Headline's policy is to use papers that are natural, renewable and recyclable products and
made from wood grown in sustainable forests. The logging and manufacturing processes
are expected to conform to the environmental regulations of the country of origin.

HEADLINE PUBLISHING GROUP
An Hachette UK Company
Carmelite House
50 Victoria Embankment
London EC4Y 0DZ

www.headline.co.uk
www.hachette.co.uk

**This journal is dedicated to you
and your future. Start where you are.**

Contents

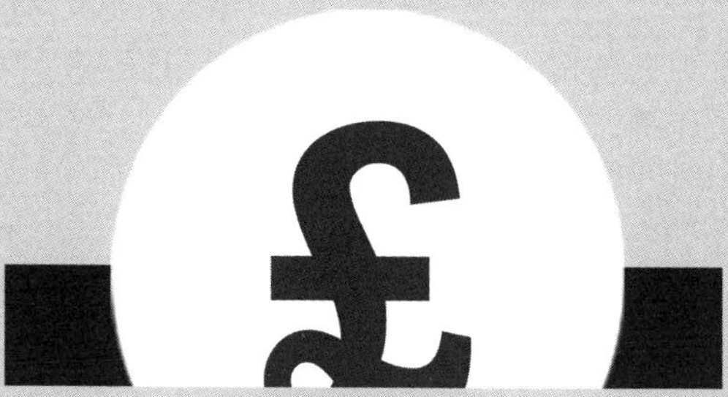

Introduction

Welcome to *The Real Life Money Journal*. You may have picked this up because you're looking for a way to tackle debt or save for something significant, or simply because you want to stop living from payday to payday. You may have picked it up because you recognise that your relationship with money isn't quite where you want it to be, and you feel like it's time to change that. Perhaps you have read my first book, *Real Life Money*, or followed the @myfrugalyear Instagram account, and are ready to put what you've learned into practice. Or maybe you've never heard of me before, and you were just looking for something slightly different from your everyday budget planner – something that acknowledges the need for deeper work on your money mindset. However you got here, welcome. We have some work to do.

Time to start thinking about money in the context of your whole, real life

Money is something that we all have to navigate in our adult lives, and yet our education in personal finance is usually patchy at best. The mindset each of us has towards money is often left to unfurl on its own, unshaped by a formal curriculum. It's influenced by our parents, our household finances growing up, and whether anyone is actually willing to talk to us about money. It's affected by the careers we choose, the goals we have, any partner with whom we might share our lives, and whether or not we have children. And, more often than not, it dictates some of those things, too.

Money is important, but not in the sense that amassing wealth should be everyone's primary focus in life. Nor is it more important than any of life's other currencies, like health, time or bonds with other people. It's important as a tool for building the life that you want. Crucially, while money itself can't make you happy, a lack of money or a fraught financial situation can make you extremely *unhappy*.

Your financial situation is not something that runs in parallel with your wider life, but something that underpins every decision and every opportunity. It's only right that your financial plans are completely bespoke to you, because there is no one-size-fits-all regime to get you to where you want to be. Nuance is something that's missing from an awful lot of financial literature, but it's important here, because sometimes it's the difference between a system that actually works for you, and one that categorically doesn't.

How to use this journal

Despite offering structure, this journal is not a prescription. There may be sections that you don't feel apply to you, or sections where you need to continue writing on extra paper. You might want to leave a certain part and return to it later, or keep coming back and adding more. The important thing is to always be honest, because that's the only way this will work. This is not the place for rounding income up and outgoings down (a habit of mine for years), and this is not a book to be abandoned the second you slip up (because you probably will, and it's absolutely fine if you do). Its function is to be a companion and guide to you while you fix your relationship with money; a firm hand-hold, rather than a judging pair of eyes.

The first couple of sections are full of prompts and guided steps for dealing with the deeper elements of any financial difficulty you're having, and give you space to explore your financial situation. Later sections will help you to build a practical plan of attack to regain control of your finances. You might choose to read the book all the way through before you begin, but it's not necessarily meant to be completed in a linear way – you should feel free to hop backwards and forwards as often as you need to. There may be pages that grow more dog-eared than others over time as you work out how to use this resource in the way that is most valuable to you, and that's OK. In fact, it's more than OK – it's the perfect way to do things.

There may be times, while delving into the depths of any financial anxiety or feelings of low self-worth, that it all gets a bit too much. When that happens, it's absolutely fine to close this book and put it down – just make sure you pick it up again.

A note on the coronavirus pandemic

When I wrote *Real Life Money*, the big, bad economic uncertainty lurking around the corner was Brexit. But then, in the early spring of 2020, the coronavirus pandemic hit. With tens of thousands of lives lost in the UK alone, and a national lockdown resulting in economic turmoil, the financial landscape for many individuals, couples and families changed suddenly and dramatically. As I write this, we have just received the news that the UK is officially in recession, with scores of job losses already and many more to come. While the support measures put in place by the government – including the unprecedented (it's the only word for it, sorry) furlough scheme – provided a safety net for a lot of people, many more fell through the cracks, suddenly finding themselves reliant on universal credit or having to live off savings. People have found their finances impacted in myriad ways: some have remained employed on a full salary and actually saved money on commuting and childcare costs; others, who were less than a year into their self-employed careers, immediately lost all of their income. Similarly, spending behaviour changed for many, from those who discovered that they were spending less without the temptation of physical shops and impromptu meals out, to those who found that anxiety, uncertainty or even boredom were causing them to spend more online.

Many who have been left financially worse off are understandably angry and upset, while those who have saved money during this time are plagued with guilt about benefitting from such a horrible set of circumstances. The ripple effects of this global catastrophe will be felt for a long time to come, so it's important to address those feelings here.

Has the pandemic affected your financial situation? If so, how has it left you feeling?

....

....

....

....

....

....

....

....

....

....

....

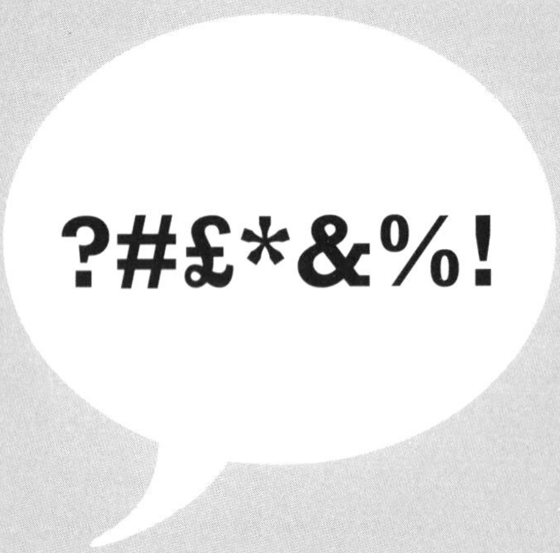

Chapter One
Your Money Story

In order to understand how you can go about fixing your relationship with money, you need to get to the bottom of how this relationship was damaged, and why that is. What happened during the course of your childhood and early adulthood that got you to this point? What shaped your current mindset? What mistakes have you made, and why did you make them? What about your current situation is due to decisions you have made, and what isn't?

I have a theory that everybody's relationship with money is comprised of five different components: Character, Background, Privilege, Attitude and Circumstances. Some of these things we can change; others, we have little control over. But if you can make a commitment to making the changes that are within your power, and doing your best to mitigate against those things it is possible to mitigate against, you will begin to see a real, material shift in your money story.

My money story

My own money story is as complex and fraught with emotion as anyone's. In the spring of 2019, I found myself with over £27,000 of credit card, store card and overdraft debt, and it was taking a toll on every area of my life: my mental health, my career, my relationships and my sense of self-worth. I was constantly juggling small amounts of money from one account to another, trying to cover all of the essentials alongside climbing minimum repayments. Then one day in mid-March, I hit a wall. I had fallen into an unarranged overdraft and there was just no money left with which I could plug the hole. After a conversation with an advisor at my bank, who did me the kindness of refunding some charges, which just about brought me back to within my limit, I sat down and finally added up what I owed.

As I embarked on a journey to pay off my debt and achieve financial security for myself and my family, I realised that just doing the sums and forcing myself to stick to a strict budget wasn't going to be enough. It occurred to me that my woeful financial situation was actually the result of years of spending beyond my means; that I had always seen available credit as an extension of my budget; and that my money mindset had been broken since early adulthood. Some of that must come down to my natural character – I've always been a bit head-in-the-clouds, not too hung up on details (although I definitely included 'great attention to detail' in the 'personal attributes' section of my CV for a good five years), and impatient. But some of it must also be attributed to my upbringing. When I thought about my financial past in more detail, I started to join the dots between what I saw growing up between two different households, each with very different attitudes towards money, and the way that I went on to spend money as an adult. I realised that, to some degree, I had always been waiting for the next bailout, and I understood how privileged I was that it had always seemed to arrive just in time. For years, my financial plan consisted of simply assuming that things would be OK when I had more money – when I earned more, when I stopped having to pay so much for childcare, when I won the lottery (yes, seriously). It was not what you could call a winning mindset. I made bad decision after bad decision – but more than that, the act of spending money became an emotional crutch for me. I would use purchases to assuage my anxiety, to cheer myself up, to quell boredom, to ward off loneliness; and also to impress others, to show people that I loved them, to try and make myself more likeable. None of those underlying issues disappear just because you make a budget – and that's why this journal exists.

Now that you've heard some of mine – and there's plenty more to share with you later – it's almost time for you to start exploring your own money story. Before you do, though, I'd urge you to take a moment and just check in with how you're feeling at this point. Make sure you do this in your own time.

'Make sure you do this in your own time.'

Guilt and shame

Both of these emotions play a big part in our attitudes towards money, and can influence how we earn, how we spend and how we save – but we often don't talk about them. Shame, in particular, likes to hide in the dark, plaguing us at the times when we are most vulnerable, like when we're already upset, or when we're on the brink of sleep. Guilt tends to be less severe, and far more short-lived. The relationship between the two, as I see it, is that shame often occurs where guilt isn't dealt with appropriately or in good enough time, and is then allowed to become absorbed deep into our consciousness.

'Shame is a focus on self; guilt is a focus on behaviour. Shame is "I am bad". Guilt is "I did something bad".'

Brené Brown
'Listening to Shame' TED Talk

Guilt

With regards to money, guilt usually occurs when we've overspent or temporarily lost our grip on our finances, or even sometimes when we perceive that we've 'wasted' money that we were actually completely justified in spending. Women, in particular, tend to feel guilty for spending money on themselves, even if they can afford it.

Can you think about a time (or times) when you've felt guilty about spending too much or not saving enough? Is that feeling justified, or are you just being hard on yourself? Explore those feelings of guilt here:

Shame

Shame is often a lot more difficult to resolve than guilt, because it usually goes right to the core of how we feel about ourselves as people. Letting go of the shame around poor financial decisions that we might have made in the past is essential in order for us to move on and build a positive relationship with money. Dealing with our feelings of shame also makes it much easier for us to open up conversations with banks and creditors, as well as family and those closest to us, which we'll look at in more detail in the next chapter. However, it's something that is much, much easier said than done, and it might take some time to get those feelings under control. Here are a few examples of things that you might feel ashamed about with regards to money:

- **having debt**
- **not having savings**
- **having buried your head in the sand or ignored your finances up to this point**
- **being seen as being shallow or materialistic because of your overspending**
- **having wasted money**
- **letting your friends, family, partner or children down**
- **having to ask for help**
- **earning well but still struggling financially**
- **not being able to afford the same lifestyle as your peers**

Shame is an emotion that thrives in the dark, but tends to shrink back when we shine a light on it. Getting those feelings out in the open is the first step towards diminishing the shame that you're feeling down to a manageable level, so try to write about your shame here. This can be a really tough part of the journey, so make sure you're feeling ready.

....

....

....

....

....

....

....

....

....

....

....

....

....

....

....

It's worth noting here that shame is an incredibly complex emotion, and is often central to mental health struggles. It may be that there are deeper elements to the shame that you are feeling that require more than journalling in order to be fully resolved. For some mental health resources, please see page 76.

Your current financial wellbeing

Before we start looking back at your money story, it's a good idea to get a rough picture of the current state of affairs – your material financial situation and how you feel about it. This means checking all of your account balances, and checking in with yourself. You might feel OK about this or, like I was, you might be terrified at the thought of finding out what the actual damage is. It can be scary, but it's crucial – you can't really start until you know where you are.

Current account balance(s)

....

Current total debt

....

Current total savings/investments/assets

....

....

How do you feel looking at those numbers? Do you feel overwhelmed? Frightened? Hopeful? Relieved? Remember that, now you know them, you can do something about them.

....

....

....

You might like to think in a bit more detail about the current state of your financial wellbeing. Are money worries affecting your sleep or your relationships? How often do you think about money? You might feel like you're constantly walking on a tightrope, trying to balance everything in order to make your salary stretch to the end of the month. You might be aware that you tend to bury your head in the sand by the time it gets to the middle of the month. Explore that here:

Exploring your financial blind spots

Many of us have particular financial blind spots: places where we don't seem to be able to control our spending; cracks in the hull where money seems to leak out with alarming speed and consistency, in a way that feels out of our control.

It can feel really hard to shine a light on these areas, but it's absolutely key to creating a better financial future – after all, if you don't know they're there, how can you mitigate against them?

One of the best ways to do this is to look back through your bank statements to see if there are any frequent transactions that weren't on your radar. It might be that you are a serial offender for signing up to free trials and then forgetting to cancel the subscription, or that you don't tend to include gifts for other people when working out your budget. Think about what your financial blind spots are, and write them down in the boxes here. You might also want to write a few words about why you think these particular areas are challenging for you:

What affordability means to you

The meaning of the word 'affordable' has changed for me over the last couple of years. Before I started changing my attitude towards money, I thought that I could afford something as long as I had the cash for it in my account, or the space on my credit card. But really, affordability is more linked to your priorities than it is to your available balance. In re-evaluating what we consider to be affordable, we need to decide what's more important to us – instant gratification or long-term security. Before I changed my mindset around money, I would feel confused when friends and colleagues spoke about their savings, and then in the same breath said that they couldn't afford a holiday this year. The reason was, of course, that the money they were saving was allocated to something else that was higher on their priority list. Now, when I'm deciding whether or not I can afford something, I ask myself the following questions:

- **Are there any upcoming costs that I'd struggle to meet if I make this purchase?**
- **Would this money be better spent elsewhere, or saved for a bigger purpose?**
- **Does the thing that I want to buy hold long-term value for me? (See chapter 4 for more on this).**

Think about what affordability means to you, or what is has meant to you in the past:

....

....

....

....

Now think about how that needs to change if you're going to achieve your long-term financial goals:

....

....

....

....

....

....

....

....

Normalise saying 'I can't afford that right now'

When you turn down Friday night drinks, a meal out or a group holiday, you're not necessarily saying that you don't have the money in your account – you're saying that you have different priorities right now. If your friends are used to you saying 'yes' to things, this change might come as a bit of a shock to them initially (see chapter 2 for more detail on how to handle this kind of conversation), but be consistent and they'll probably come around.

Looking back

Now is a good time to start thinking about how and why things started to go wrong. Can you remember how things were for you when you were growing up? Did your parents or caregivers ever speak to you about money, and if so, how did they talk about it? What were their attitudes towards money? Did they have any money hang-ups of their own? What, if any, financial education did you get at school? Was there anything about money that confused you when you were young?

....

....

....

....

....

....

This exercise may have shed some light on a few things, or you may still be in the dark about why money is difficult for you. Personally, I can barely remember a time when money didn't make me feel some level of anxiety or discomfort – even (and possibly especially) at times when I was spending it with reckless abandon. Can you remember when you first felt worried about money? Perhaps you could think about how your feelings around money have evolved with time, experience and responsibilities – how events in your life have shaped both your attitude towards money, and your material financial circumstances. Take all the time and space you need to explore your own journey with money, and the reasons behind it. Use extra paper if you need to.

....

....

....

....

....

....

....

....

....

....

....

....

....

....

....

Discovering the causes of your financial difficulties, and coming to terms with those causes, is an important step in the journey towards financial stability and wellbeing. After all, it's far more difficult to break toxic habits if you don't know why you developed them in the first place.

Your turning point

It may be that there was no particular flash point for you; no particular reason you decided to pick up this journal, or to start looking at your relationship with money in closer detail. For many people, it's a gradual process of coming to the realisation that things need to change; for some, it's a sudden change in circumstances; and for others, it's a particular event or shock to the system. Mine was a telephone conversation with my bank. The advisor was asking me why I was still in an unarranged overdraft after a couple of notifications. All I could say was, 'There's just . . . no money left.'

By the time I hung up the phone, I knew that I needed to get a grasp on things. We were running out of time to fix our situation without entering into a formal arrangement, and my partner and I were both about to start new jobs with slightly higher salaries. It seemed like a bit of a now-or-never moment. Looking back now, it feels like that moment of realisation was the axis on which the whole of the rest of our lives pivoted. Needless to say, I'm so grateful that it happened.

You might find it helpful to write about your own turning point here.

....

....

....

....

....

....

....

Start where you are

It's all any of us can do. It might be that this chapter has made you realise that your relationship with money is a little (or a lot) more broken than you thought it was, or you might feel relieved to finally be able to join some of the dots and discover the reasons behind your struggles. You might have found assessing and writing down your current financial situation difficult or distressing, but please don't let any of these things put you off – because starting to fix this now, today, will be much better than waiting until you feel like the time is right. In my experience, that perfect moment can be quite elusive.

When I was younger, I had quite a difficult relationship with food. (I would put money on there being a correlation between people who struggle with money and those who struggle with food, but I'm not nearly clever or important enough to do a proper study.) I would often want to wait until I'd got down to a certain weight in order to properly 'start' working on my relationship with food. I was scared to step on the scales and be presented with a number that felt overwhelming to me, so I wanted to try to lose weight before finding out how much I actually weighed. Thankfully, my body image issues are now largely resolved, but at one point, I felt the same way about money. I wanted to wait until more of my debt was paid off before taking a proper look at how much I owed, because the thought of knowing the numbers as they stood right then terrified me. I thought that if I just held on a little bit longer, I could reduce my card balances enough to 'properly get started' on paying off my debts. In reality, I was just blindly lurching forwards without really knowing where I was heading. The truth is that until you add up those totals and get a solid idea of where you are now, there's little hope of being able to turn things around.

Your motivation

In every area of our lives, we each have things that motivate and propel us forwards: things that we keep in mind when making plans and decisions. We'll explore setting goals and working towards them in more detail later on, but now is a really great moment to put a marker down and think about your reasons for wanting to get yourself on to a better financial footing, once and for all. Bearing in mind that our financial wellbeing is very much part of our overall wellbeing, and that money worries seep into lots of other areas of our lives, remember that these reasons don't really have to be strictly finance-related – they might be to do with how you feel, your relationships or your future. Establishing your motivations and priorities now gives you something to refer back to when other things threaten to take over, or when the process of building financial security feels like too long a slog. They're your reason to keep going at times when you feel like giving up.

For example, my own core motivations around money have always been:

1. To protect my mental health and emotional wellbeing.

2. To build a financially secure future for my children.

3. To have a chance of owning a home one day.

Have a think about what motivates you, and fill the three spaces below:

1.
....

2.
....

3.
....

It's probably not all your fault

Accountability is important in successfully tackling any issue in life, but it's very easy for us to slip into self-flagellation if we're not careful. For most of us, there will be elements in our financial histories that were outside of our control – things that influenced our income or outgoings that we had no power over. In the same way that it helps to look at how your decisions and behaviour have affected your financial life, it's also important to acknowledge and accept the external factors, rather than carrying the weight of every setback on your conscience. At least some elements of your financial precariousness are likely to be a result of illness, redundancy or some other *force majeure* (particularly in post-pandemic society). You need to be able to separate the aspects that are within your control from those parts that were simply not your fault.

If it's helpful, you might like to explore some of these external factors below. It's OK to feel bitter or upset or hard done by, but you might find you feel better after getting some of these feelings down on paper.

....

....

....

....

....

....

....

....

The power of reflection

I hope that this first section has given you the chance to reflect on your own, unique relationship with money. In throwing open the doors and sweeping the cobwebs from those dark and murky corners, perhaps you have gained some insights into what needs to change going forwards. I have always found there's something uniquely cathartic in finally getting all of those money worries and feelings down on paper, and that it's helpful in empowering you to start moving on.

'It's OK to feel bitter or upset or hard done by, but you might find you feel better after getting some of these feelings down on paper.'

Five minutes with Emilie Bellet

Emilie is the author of personal finance manifesto *You're Not Broke, You're Pre-Rich* and founder of Vestpod, a digital platform and community that inspires and educates women to be more confident and competent with money. She has a corporate finance background, but keeps everything simple, digestible and empowering.

What do you consider the unique financial challenges facing women to be?
Women have a very different work pattern compared to men and this has a direct impact on how much money we earn and save. We'll earn less money over the course of our careers, not only because of the gender pay gap, but also because we might stop working or go part-time in order to take care of children or ageing parents. Plus, we live longer, so we need extra money for retirement (which won't be our easiest or most affordable time of life). On top of all that, women invest less than men, so we don't see our long-term savings and pensions grow as much as they should.

As for financial decision-making, although we've traditionally been in charge of household budgeting, most of us are still taking a step back when it comes to important decisions about investing and long-term financial planning.

If someone is looking to take control of their finances, what do you consider to be the most important thing they should do, before anything else?
Through running Vestpod and writing *You're Not Broke, You're Pre-Rich*, I've learned that your 'money mindset' is a complicated and super-important thing to understand if you're

going to get better at money management. No one is 'good' or 'bad' with money. We just build habits and beliefs over time that have an impact on the way we manage our finances.

Acknowledging your relationship with money; talking more about money; opening your eyes to the reality of your current situation – these are the best starting points. Then you can face financial planning, educating yourself and navigating the financial landscape. We can all do it!

Do you have any tips for someone who wants to break out of a financial rut, whether they're battling to pay off debt, struggling to save or limping through to the end of each month? For me, it's all about taking small steps. You're not going to completely change your financial situation overnight, but you can start building healthier financial habits. Motivation is a big part of the equation. Money creates a lot of stress and anxiety and, as we all know, it's easy to feel ashamed of your financial position.

Too often, money is associated with self-worth. So first off, understand that you are worth much more than just the money you have in the bank, and then take active steps to make things run more smoothly. Could you change the way you talk to yourself? Try being as kind and positive as you would be if talking to a friend who was having money troubles. Identify and change your negative thought patterns. And, most importantly, stop comparing yourself to others.

Once you've let go of all that destructive emotion, you'll find it easier to begin making a plan to repay debts and start to save, because you'll see it as just developing a skill or a new habit, like learning to drive or swim, rather than an intrinsic problem with your personality that you have to change. You'll get there!

Chapter Two
Difficult Conversations

For most of us, the ideal scenario would be to simply fix our financial woes behind closed doors, without having to admit to our mistakes or say those numbers out loud. I know so well how it feels to be embarrassed and ashamed of your financial situation, pretending to colleagues that you're planning a summer holiday or saving for a house when you're actually skimming along the very bottom of your overdraft, or just going along with Friday-night drinks, praying that your credit card doesn't get declined, because you can't bear to utter the words, 'I can't afford it'. I know what it's like to find yourself skirting around cashflow issues with your bank when they call to discuss an unarranged overdraft or returned direct debit, or refusing to pick up the phone at all because you just can't face explaining it. The cruel irony is that, for many of us, if we could only bring ourselves to have these conversations, they can lead to things that might materially help us. Being open and honest about my finances, after years of keeping everything to myself, was not only hugely beneficial for my mental and emotional wellbeing; it also opened the door to practical solutions that I'd never imagined would be possible.

When we keep information to ourselves, we perpetuate the shame that we feel around it. The shame you feel about your financial situation then becomes layered with the added shame of perceived deception, and you feel even worse. It's also worth noting that if other people aren't aware of how difficult things are, it's much easier to bury your head in the sand and not feel the need to take positive action.

Hopefully, now that you have a better understanding of where things went wrong, and why, you might feel a little more comfortable opening up to others. It may take a little while, but planning those conversations can really help you to feel more confident and prepared when the time comes.

Not everybody will understand

In an ideal world, the people around us would listen to what we have to say and react in a rational and empathetic way, but we, as a society, are still very funny about money. How we manage our personal finances is often moralised, with unfair and untrue connotations about our characters and values being attached to debt, overspending or financial difficulty. Even those closest to us may have some preconceptions about people who struggle to manage their money, and this can be difficult to deal with.

If you put yourself out there and are faced with judgement or disapproval, it's important to try and let it go. Whether it's a stern advisor from your bank or a grandparent who just doesn't understand, you don't need to internalise their reaction and use it as yet another stick with which to beat yourself – it's important to remember that the reason you're even having this conversation is because you've made a commitment to turning things around.

Opening up to family and friends

How much you need or want to confide in your family and friends is completely up to you, and it will depend on your individual financial situation and unique relationships with the people in your life. If you're using this journal because you recognise a need to feel more in control of your finances, but aren't in any particular financial difficulty, it might just be that you want to discuss your priorities with your friends, or that you'd like to have a more open dialogue about money with your partner. But if you're facing financial challenges that are affecting your wellbeing, or if you've been keeping your money worries to yourself, these conversations might be more about asking for support, or finally laying your cards down on the table.

'Hopefully, now that you have a better understanding of where things went wrong, and why, you might feel a little more comfortable opening up to others.'

Imagining the conversation

Often, when we think about opening up to those closest to us about our finances, we imagine the worst-case scenario for their reaction. In my experience, the reality is very rarely as bad as what we've been picturing. Think about the people you want to discuss this with, and how you worry they might react. This might be a partner not taking things seriously enough, more financially secure friends judging you, or family members being disappointed in you – whatever's playing on your mind. What are some of the reactions you're afraid of hearing?

Now, think about what your response might be to those reactions. Often, when we're put on the spot or when we're hurt by a statement, it can disorientate us and prevent us from responding in an appropriate or constructive way. The main purpose of this conversation is to get on the same page and eventually be in a position to move forward, so it's good to have a plan for what you're going to say. This might be a sincere apology, an explanation, reassurance that you are dealing with things, an indication of any progress you've made so far, or even a challenge to their attitude.

Now that you've thought about the kind of reactions you're worried about getting, it might be helpful to work up a kind of script to use for these discussions, first outlining the points that you want to get across, and then drafting out how the conversation might go. This will help you to feel more prepared, even if it's fairly vague.

Important information to get across:

You: ....

....

Them: ....

....

You: ....

....

Them: ....

....

You: ....

....

Them: ....

....

Of course, it might be that you would find it easier to write things down in the form of a letter or note, especially if you're worried about losing your thread (or your nerve). If this is your chosen option, you can use this space to draft your letter:

....

....

....

....

....

....

....

....

....

....

....

....

....

....

How do you feel now?

It's completely normal for there to be an emotional aftermath to these conversations, and often the feelings are quite mixed and complicated. Use the space below to write freely about your experience of opening up. What was difficult? What was positive? How do you feel about moving forwards now? Were there any frustrations? Use extra paper if you need to.

....

....

....

....

....

....

....

....

....

....

....

....

....

....

....

....

....

....

....

....

....

....

....

....

Don't forget, at this point, to give yourself a bit of credit for doing something immensely difficult. We're all conditioned to keep our financial matters to ourselves and not to admit when we're struggling, so if you've managed to overcome that, you should be proud. Write something nice about yourself here:

....

....

....

Setting new boundaries

One of the outcomes of your conversations may have been the realisation that you need to set some new boundaries in your relationships in order to protect your financial and emotional health. For many of us, a lot of our overspending is caused by a desire to please people, a wish not to let others down, or just because it's easier to say yes. There is often a tug of war when it comes to our financial priorities, but if all or part of the cause of that is external pressure from people in your life, then it's time to look at enforcing some limitations on how much you allow these people to influence you.

How you set your own boundaries is very personal to you, especially when it comes to money. There's an odd dichotomy whereby we often clam up when the subject of money comes up in conversation, but also absorb the views and opinions of others and allow them to cloud our judgement – even when they're not directed at us. Learning to safeguard your own approach to personal finance from the judgement and criticism of others is an important step in reaching your goals. This might mean saying no to a friend who is pressuring you to join them on an expensive holiday, ensuring that you and your partner have an equal say in household spending, or simply refusing to let anybody else make you feel bad about money.

List any new boundaries that you need to set below, along with one or more reasons why you need to set them. These might pertain to a particular person/people, or they might just be general in nature.

Boundary:

....

....

Reason:

....

....

Boundary: ....

....

Reason: ....

....

Boundary: ....

....

Reason: ....

....

Boundary: ....

....

Reason: ....

....

Sometimes, people will resist respecting your boundaries, because they are used to having a certain amount of access to you and influence on your decisions. Often, your lack of boundaries will have been beneficial to them in the past, so it's natural that they might put up a bit of a fight, or not understand to begin with. Stay firm, and they'll soon get used to the new dynamic. Once cemented, mutually understood boundaries can actually strengthen your bond.

Speaking to your bank and creditors

When you're dealing with a difficult or precarious financial situation, it's also important to keep open the line of communication with your bank and/or creditors. There was a time when the thought of having a conversation with my bank would send shivers down my spine. I would only ever call them if it was absolutely necessary, and I'd brace myself for an interrogation into every penny I'd spent (which never came). The more money I owed on my credit cards, the less willing I was to pick up the phone to them to discuss my interest options – most of the time, I just wanted to forget they existed. The problem is that the more you avoid engaging, the more anxious you're going to be about the letters, emails and texts that you receive, and you also risk missing important information about things like interest rates and fee changes if you can't bring yourself to read them.

The good news is that once you get into the habit of being in regular communication with your financial providers, those phone calls start to feel less daunting. Once I had made a plan for how I was going to repay my debt and get on top of my finances, I called all of my creditors to see if there was anything they could do to help me, without me having to commit to a formal repayment arrangement. Gestures of good will – which can include things like refunding or freezing interest, lowering interest rates or refunding fees – vary from provider to provider, and are usually available based on different sets of rules. It's all quite opaque, and I've definitely found some banks and lenders to be more helpful and sympathetic than others, but it's always worth an enquiry.

If you have some worries about these calls, use the space opposite to air and explore them. Remember that the advisors on the other end of the line are human beings, too, and their job is to help, rather than to judge you. I often hear from people who work in the finance sector but still struggle with managing their own financial situation, so there's no reason to assume that they will chastise or speak down to you. They spend their working day speaking to different people dealing with a whole range of financial situations, so there's no need to be embarrassed. If you find that the person you're speaking to isn't being very understanding, you can always ask to speak to somebody else.

....

....

....

....

....

....

....

....

....

....

....

....

....

....

....

Before you pick up the phone to your bank, it's really good to have an idea of what they could do that would help you. Calling with a specific aim – whether that's getting some financial advice, having overdraft fees refunded, reducing the interest rate on your credit card or discussing a more formal payment arrangement – will help you to navigate the conversation. Use this space to outline what you'd like to get out of a conversation with your bank or credit provider.

....

....

....

....

Some other important things to have set up before you make the call are:

- **a glass of water or a hot drink (or both)**
- **all of your account details and passwords – this will stop you from feeling flustered before you've even started talking**
- **a fully charged phone, if calling from a mobile – the last thing you want to do is run out of battery and then have to explain everything all over again**
- **some free time – it's best not to try and do this while looking after your children or juggling other tasks**

Use the box opposite to make notes during your conversation – sometimes there's a lot of information to take in, and jotting things down will make things clearer. It might also help you to prepare for your next call.

Seeking help elsewhere

If you've found that neither the people in your life nor your bank can offer you the support that you're looking for right now, it may be that you need to reach out to a specialist service that can help you to figure out your options. There are organisations that have been set up specifically to help those dealing with debt and financial challenges, and all are free of charge, so please be wary of the manipulative marketing for costly debt-management companies that may spring up on your social media feeds or in website ads the moment you type anything about debt into Google. Many of these companies target women with emotive messaging around being a better mum or similar, preying on people in desperate situations – but there is always free help available.

Some places you might look for help are:

StepChange Debt Charity – stepchange.org
Christians Against Poverty – capuk.org
The Money Advice Service – moneyadviceservice.org.uk
Citizens Advice – citizensadvice.org.uk

Again, before getting in touch with any of these organisations, it's a really good idea to have at least a rough vision for what you'd like to gain from speaking to them. You can make notes about this here.

....

....

....

....

....

Again, you'll probably want to make notes on your options when speaking to any of these services, or even when browsing their websites. Use this space to jot things down in:

....

....

....

Remember to take some time to consider your options – you don't have to commit to any one course of action the first time that you reach out.

Take some time to reflect

Breaking your silence around debt or money worries can be very challenging and emotionally taxing, and you might be feeling a bit strange – particularly if you've been keeping this to yourself for an extended period of time. Use this space to explore how you feel now that you've spoken up – do you feel relieved? Comforted? Raw? Empowered? Do you feel optimistic, or has it just dawned on you how much work there is to do? Take the time you need to explore those feelings, and use extra paper if you need to.

....

....

....

....

Chapter Three
Mental Health

Thankfully, after decades of silence, repressed feelings and misunderstood illnesses, the mental health conversation has picked up steam in the last decade. Many public figures now speak openly about their struggles with anxiety and depression and the ways in which they cope; the subject is discussed extensively on social media, and there are more support networks available. That's not to say that there isn't still a stigma attached to certain diagnoses and symptoms, but generally, we're more open. Money, and the effect that it can have on your mental health, is often left out of mainstream narratives, despite being a major cause of mental health issues.

In fact, the relationship between financial difficulties and poor mental health is a reciprocal one. According to the Money and Mental Health Policy Institute, almost half (forty-six per cent) of people with problem debt also experience mental health problems, while almost a fifth of people with a mental health condition (eighteen per cent) have problem debt. (Problem debt is a term used to describe a situation where a person is unable to afford their debt repayments.) It's easy to see how the feelings of shame and anxiety stirred up by money problems can incite or exacerbate poor mental health, and it's also understandable that good money management can fall by the wayside when a person is struggling with their mental health.

I have a diagnosed anxiety disorder, flare-ups of which have historically corresponded with my financial troubles. When things were really bad – when the money consistently ran out mid-month and I was plagued by unarranged overdraft texts and struggling to make repayments on huge credit card balances – I was in a heightened state of anxiety almost all the time, dealing with symptoms ranging from intrusive thoughts to chest pains and blurry vision. I also experienced periods of incredibly low mood, where the thought of something as simple as making a cup of coffee or having a shower made me want to cry. At these times, it was as much as I could do to look after the most basic of my physical needs, let alone my financial ones. I blamed myself for the fact that things were so difficult, not really taking into account the external factors at play, and got trapped in a cycle of self-loathing that made it very difficult to function – and even harder to be happy. As things started to get better financially, and I started feeling more in control, my mood lifted. It didn't happen overnight, and I actually found that the process of confronting my debt temporarily made me feel more anxious, like bubbles rising to the surface before dissipating – but slowly, money stopped having such a hold over how I felt and what I thought about myself. One day, I woke up, and I realised that I felt better. Not completely fixed, but better.

How does money affect your mental health?

Think about how money affects your mental health. Fill the brain below with some words that spring to mind.

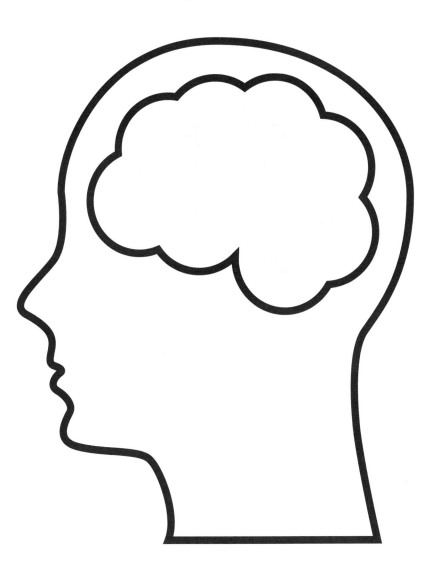

Look at the words you wrote in the brain. Can you expand on these a little? Are there any particular situations that exacerbate feelings of anxiety or low mood? For example, I would often dread checking my bank balance. But the longer I put it off, the more anxious I would feel about checking it, and it would cause me to spiral. Is there anything like this in your own behaviour that you can recognise and describe?

....

....

....

....

....

....

....

....

....

'It's normal to worry about money, but it's not healthy to worry about it all the time.'

Tips for protecting your mental health when dealing with financial difficulty

• It's normal to worry about money, but it's not healthy to worry about it all the time. Try allocating a certain time during the day for worrying. During this time, you can allow yourself to worry, but try to stop it from filtering out of this time and into every waking moment.

• Breathing exercises can really help when dealing with anxiety. There are resources available on the NHS website, and apps like Headspace have tools for meditation.

• Move your body. Exercise can be one of the most useful tools in your kit for managing financial worry, but it doesn't have to mean buying expensive sports equipment or paying for a gym membership. Dancing in your living room will raise your heart rate and give you a kick of endorphins, if you're enthusiastic enough. Author Bella Mackie talks about running for anxiety brilliantly in her book *Jog On: How Running Saved My Life*.

• Make sure that you are sleeping properly, eating well and drinking enough water. If sleep doesn't come easily, try to avoid screens for a while before bed – and don't let sleep become another way of putting pressure on yourself.

Mind how you talk to yourself

Being able to critique our own past behaviour and see where we've made wrong turns is an important part of letting go of toxic habits and building better ones, but we also need to be aware of the danger of being too hard on ourselves. Not every thought we have about ourselves is true, and sometimes it's difficult to differentiate between legitimate constructive criticism and negative self-talk that's detrimental to our progress. This is something that I still have to actively monitor in order to protect my own mental health, and will probably have to continue to be mindful of for years to come – possibly always. Old habits die hard, and when you're used to self-flagellating at every given opportunity, it can be difficult to actually give yourself credit for what you're getting right. In our society, we put so much emphasis on money and possessions as a measure of success that it can feel as though we're failing at everything when we don't quite get it right with our finances.

Words like 'irresponsible', 'materialistic', 'silly' and 'frivolous' often get floated around with regards to overspending or mismanaging money, and we tend to internalise these and use them as sticks with which to beat ourselves, which isn't good for us. Every time one of these thoughts pops into your head, write it down below – and then? Cross. It. Out. Thinking negative things about yourself will only perpetuate the idea that you can't do this, when you absolutely can.

....

....

....

....

....

Affirmations

In getting rid of some of the negative things we say to ourselves, we create space for positive thoughts to exist – but often they won't materialise on their own, which is why affirmations can come in handy. Affirmations are basically things that you say to yourself to remind you of all of the ways in which you are strong, capable and equal to whatever challenges come your way. Having a series of affirmations that you can come back to when you slip up or start to doubt yourself can be the difference between sliding backwards or picking yourself up, dusting yourself off and carrying on. It's best to say them out loud, which can feel strange and unnatural at first – especially if you're not used to having anything nice to say to or about yourself – but you don't have to shout them through a loudspeaker: you can start by muttering them under your breath, then slowly build up to saying them in a clear, confident voice.

Here are a few examples to try:

- **I successfully manage responsibilities in other areas of my life, so I am more than capable of being in control of my finances.**
- **I learn from my mistakes.**
- **I am more than my financial situation.**
- **I control the things that I can.**
- **I am going to be so proud of myself when I see this through.**
- **I am more than what I earn, what I own and what I owe.**

Now write a few of your own. Think about your good qualities, the things that you've achieved and what you've done right. Add to them as you progress.

....

....

....

Affordable self-care

For something so simple in theory, the subject of taking care of ourselves has been heavily overcomplicated and commercialised in recent years. We've had it drummed into us that we can actually buy a feeling of general wellbeing, with lotions and potions and workshops and scented candles; but really, it's the small, everyday acts that tend to make a real difference. It took me a long time to realise that the reason none of the things I bought to try and fix how I was feeling weren't working was because I was neglecting the basics: things like washing off my make-up at the end of the day, going to bed early to combat the five a.m. wake-ups with my son, or drinking water when I was thirsty. All of those things that we neglect when we're tired or stressed add up, and leave us feeling like we need something big (and expensive) to compensate. So really, when you think about it, practising self-care consistently and affordably is a very good financial decision.

'So really, when you think about it, practising self-care consistently and affordably is a very good financial decision.'

Free and low-cost self-care tips

Looking after ourselves doesn't have to cost the earth – or even anything at all. Here are a few things that cost nothing, or very little:

Be mindful about what your body needs
If you're thirsty, drink a glass of water. If you're hungry, eat. If you need the loo, go straight away rather than waiting. We often get used to putting our own basic needs right at the bottom of the list – but we can't give to others if we have nothing left for ourselves.

Give yourself the gift of time
Start by trying to allocate thirty minutes, two or three times a week, where you are uncontactable. Switch off your phone and read a book, listen to music or have a bath. If this isn't possible, try to use any 'dead' time, like your commute, to do something enriching, such as reading on public transport or listening to a podcast in the car.

Use what you have
Most of us have drawers upon drawers' worth of abandoned creams and lotions that we don't use. Treat yourself to some time going through them, then set a reminder to apply hand cream or body lotion each day. Better yet, if you live with a partner, have them remind you. It's good for them to recognise the need for you to take care of yourself, too.

Stretch
Many us spend our days hunched over a computer, picking up and putting down toddlers, or sitting in the car – or some combination of the above. Doing some simple stretches or yoga moves will help you to feel more open and flexible.

Make your own self-care list

Make a list of things you need in order to feel content and cared for. They can be as basic as you like, right down to having a shower and brushing your teeth every day.

My self-care list

- ....
- ....
- ....
- ....
- ....
- ....
- ....
- ....
- ....
- ....

Now, for each of those things, think about how you can start to make sure that they actually happen – measures that you can put in place to ring-fence some time to dedicate to looking after yourself:

....

....

....

....

....

....

....

....

....

....

....

....

....

....

....

Podcasts for self-care

I mentioned listening to podcasts earlier because they have been a huge part of my self-care journey. I find that they make the most mundane of tasks – like washing up or cleaning the bathroom – more bearable, and they also provide a great soundtrack to exercise (also excellent for self-care) and travelling. Most are completely free to subscribe to, and there's such a huge variety out there that you will always find something to suit your taste.

To make you laugh

Laughter can pierce even the gloomiest of days, and act as a welcome distraction from anxiety and low mood. Here are my favourite podcasts for laugh-out-loud content:

- *Off Menu* – Comedians James Acaster and Ed Gamble interview a variety of guests about their dream menu. If you love food, that's a bonus too.

- *My Dad Wrote a Porno* – One of the most popular podcasts worldwide, but still rib-achingly funny a few seasons in. Not for the faint of heart.

- *Dear Joan and Jericha* – Also not for the faint of heart, faux agony aunts Joan (Vicki Pepperdine) and Jericha (Julia Davis) respond to ridiculous letters with even more ridiculous answers.

For self-empathy

Sometimes, hearing other people talk about their own journeys through life, the mistakes that they've made and the challenges they've faced, helps us to understand and empathise with ourselves more. These podcasts help us to gain perspective when we're in need of it:

• *How to Fail with Elizabeth Day* – Author and journalist Elizabeth Day interviews a wonderful selection of guests about their biggest failures, and how those failures have ultimately led them to success.

• *Unlocking Us with Brené Brown* – Queen of my heart Brené explores the emotions and experiences that bring meaning and purpose to our lives.

To make you think

Sometimes, our brains need stimulation in order to stay motivated and focused on our future. These podcasts are full of content that teaches us new things and makes us challenge ourselves:

• *In Good Company* – Writer and speaker Otegha Uwagba speaks to smart, successful women about life and work.

• *Is This Working?* – Journalists Tiffany Philippou and Anna Codrea-Rado speak to guests about different ways of working, and the relationship between how we live our lives and how we earn our money.

Overcoming perfectionism

It's funny, I used to think about perfectionism as a good thing. I thought that being fixated on doing everything just right meant that I'd always end up with the results I wanted, but the truth is that perfectionism is often the enemy of good mental health and financial wellbeing. The effect of it on our finances is twofold – it makes us spend more in pursuit of the perfect outfit/living room/wedding/holiday, and it also prevents us from tackling our less-than-perfect financial situation, because we can't bear to face our mistakes head-on.

Perfectionism makes it very difficult to actually get started with anything, because our natural instinct is to wait until all of the stars are aligned, until we feel confident in our ability to complete the task at hand flawlessly. In order to tackle our finances, we are going to have to make an effort to overcome our perfectionism.

Are you a perfectionist? Can you think of a time when your perfectionism has cost you financially or emotionally?

....

....

....

....

....

....

....

....

Zoe Blaskey's tips for ditching perfectionism

Zoe Blaskey is a coach and the founder of Motherkind, a support community and podcast. Perfectionism is one of her specialist subjects.

Perfectionism is often misunderstood. People often think it's what we look like or how tidy our houses are. This can be a part of perfectionism, of course, but it is far from the full picture. My definition of perfectionism is not feeling good enough.

Tip one: The easiest way to start to overcome perfectionism is to become aware of it and the impact it is having on your life. Sounds simple, doesn't it? But we can't change what we're not aware of. I suggest committing to a week of noticing your perfectionist behaviours. Grab a pen and paper and use the questions below as writing prompts:

• Where did I notice perfectionism today?
• What did it stop me doing?
• What is one small action I can take tomorrow on something I have been avoiding through perfectionism?

Tip two: Often, perfectionistic behaviour can come from listening to your inner critic – the voice that tells you you're not enough just as you. Try to create some distance from it.

Give your inner critic a name, so when you hear those harsh, critical words, you can say, 'Ah, there's [insert name]' and challenge what it is saying to you. To take this a step further, you could then replace that negative thought with a positive one. Gradually, this will help you come to see a powerful truth: you are not your thoughts.

Protecting yourself on social media

Social media can play a huge role in both our mental health and our relationships with money, so it's important that we learn to recognise when our scrolling habits are doing more harm than good. For me, when my emotional shopping was at its worst, social media – in particular Instagram – could be a real spending trigger. Depending on who we follow, our newsfeeds can sometimes appear to be a reel of perfection that we could never hope to achieve in our own lives. It makes us feel inadequate and uncomposed in comparison, because we have unprecedented access to people from a plethora of different backgrounds, who we think of as our peers without really knowing much about them. We don't know how their financial situation compares to our own, and yet we feel compelled to own the same 'it' products, go on the same holidays and style our homes in the same way.

We also need to remember that a large amount of the content that we see on social media nowadays is actually advertising, whether it's paid media served up to us by brands using various terrifying algorithms that allow social networking sites to catch us right at our most vulnerable moments, or influencer ads, which are sometimes hard to tell from organic content. It's easy, when we're caught in the scroll, not to notice when we're being advertised to, and to find ourselves seduced by the perfect images we're presented with.

That's not to say that you need to come off social media entirely – although that's definitely an option, and I'm sure there are some strong arguments for it – but being mindful of how you use it will be good for your mental and financial health.

Tips for using social media in a healthy way:

- Don't 'hate follow'. Life's too short to spend your time feeling resentful, angry or jealous.
- Avoid getting into pointless arguments. I know how tempting this is, but it's very rare that you'll actually change someone's mind, and you'll probably just find yourself feeling more and more wound up.
- Unfollow or mute people who trigger unwanted feelings or behaviour.
- Put a time limit on your scrolling. Our brains like to finish things, but you can't 'complete' Instagram: there's always more content to consume. Set your own boundaries.
- Remember that you're only seeing the highlights. Nobody's life is perfect.

'It makes us feel inadequate and uncomposed in comparison, because we have unprecedented access to people from a plethora of different backgrounds, who we think of as our peers without really knowing much about them.'

Think about the way you use social media – what do you think are the pros and cons for your financial and mental health?

Mental health pros	Mental health cons
Financial health pros	Financial health cons

Now, think about what you can do to improve the way you operate on social media. Are there any accounts that you need to unfollow or mute? List them here:

....

....

....

....

....

....

....

....

....

....

....

....

Social media can be a brilliant outlet for your creativity and a source of support in all kinds of situations – my Instagram account certainly changed my life for the better – but it can also come at a cost to our wellbeing. Look after yourself.

Creating your mental health toolkit

You may find that you can work through these feelings and put measures in place to protect your mental health through this, or you might need some help. In order to access prescribed medication or talking therapy, you will need to speak to your GP and/or self-refer to your local mental health service, but there are also charities and online resources that can help during difficult moments.

In this section, I've listed a variety of different resources and touchpoints that you can use to build your own custom money and mental health toolkit.

Websites

www.mind.org.uk
www.samaritans.org
www.thecalmzone.net
www.blurtitout.org
www.anxietyuk.org.uk

Instagram accounts

@drjennhardy
@thepsychologymum
@foodandpsych
@the_positive_planner
@therapised
@drchatterjee
@worrywellbeing

Telephone services

Samaritans: 116 123 (24 hours)

Anxiety UK: 03444 775 774
(Monday to Friday, 9.30am to 5.30pm)

Mind: 0300 123 3393 (Monday to Friday, 9am to 6pm)

Your personalised mental health toolkit

Different things work for different people, and you might need to try a few different approaches before you come up with a combination of tools and resources that give you the support that you need. Look at the resources opposite for tips and ideas, and add some of your own to build yourself a personalised toolkit, which you can use as a reference point as you work through this journal.

1

2

3

4

5

6

7

8

9

10

Knowing when to seek help

Sometimes, we reach a place where we can't seem to feel better by ourselves. My GP described it to me as being at the bottom of a steep hill with no petrol left in the tank. You can see that, at the top of the hill, there's a petrol station where you'll be able to top up your tank and continue your journey, but you need an extra boost to get you there. Sometimes, especially during particularly stressful periods, we let ourselves get too low on fuel, and need a little outside intervention – it's normal, and nothing to be ashamed of.

It can be quite difficult to recognise where the line is between feeling a normal amount of fluctuation in our mood and needing help. It can also be hard to realise when we've crossed it. Here are some things to look out for:

- **disturbed sleep**
- **lethargy**
- **a change in eating behaviours**
- **avoiding contact with people**
- **feeling unable to do simple tasks**
- **thoughts of harming yourself**
- **withdrawing from hobbies and interests**
- **continuous irritability or anxiety**
- **continuous low mood or tearfulness**

If any of these behaviours continue for more than two weeks, it's a good idea to speak to your GP, who can direct you to the appropriate services. If you need to do this, make some notes about your concerns, to make it easier to describe to your doctor.

....

....

....

Don't forget to check in with yourself – even when things are going well

As I mentioned previously, I found that, along with the positive feelings of progress, beginning the process of paying off my debt and regaining control of my finances threw up a lot of mixed emotions. When we're forced to face the mistakes that we've made in the past, or relive painful experiences that were out of our control, it's only natural that it will affect our moods. Use the space below to check in with yourself regularly on this journey, especially right at the start.

How am I feeling?

....

....

....

....

How am I feeling?

....

....

....

....

How am I feeling?

....

....

....

How am I feeling?

....

....

....

How am I feeling?

....

....

....

Money, mental health and self-esteem

We all have mental health, and we all experience its fluctuations in response to different influences. Money can provoke all kinds of unwelcome thoughts and feelings which, in turn, can affect your mental health and self-esteem in a negative way. Hopefully this section has helped you to gain a greater awareness of the relationship between how you spend and how you feel, and to notice any red flags in your feelings and behaviour that might indicate that there's some work to do.

'Money can provoke all kinds of unwelcome thoughts and feelings which, in turn, can affect your mental health and self-esteem in a negative way.'

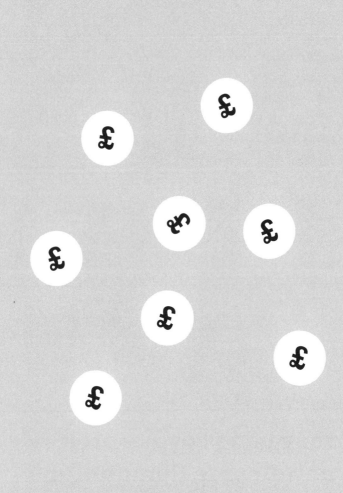

Chapter Four
Spending Mindfully

As I mentioned before, a key step in taking control of my finances was realising that it's not possible to out-earn toxic spending habits. I had always assumed that, one day, my salary would afford me all of the material possessions and experiences I desired – I just needed to get that next bonus, that next promotion. But the truth is, it just doesn't work like that. Spending beyond your means is something of a chronic condition and, certainly for me, earning more simply meant spending more.

Understanding toxic spending habits

It's crucial to get to the bottom of those problem spending habits if we're to achieve the financial peace of mind that we crave. Problem spending habits are varied: you might deliberately stop checking your bank balance mid-month, so that you don't have to see the impact of your spending on your cashflow; you could be susceptible to making impulse purchases; you may be prone to spending to try and fix a problem; you might rely heavily on credit for non-essentials; or perhaps you struggle to resist a discount. Let's start by identifying up to three spending habits that you recognise are causing you problems:

....

....

....

....

....

....

....

Can you go deeper into these habits, and think a little more about where you think they might have come from? Are they things that you have learned from a parent or caregiver? Are they coping mechanisms that you've developed in response to something? Are they connected to one another?

Use these boxes to explore the feelings around the habits you've identified, and see if you can figure out why they exist. I've included an example to get you started.

Toxic spending habit: Shopping in response to something upsetting me or something not going to plan.

· We often used to go shopping to escape difficult situations at home when I was younger.
· The cultural trope of 'retail therapy'.
· There's a feeling of release when completing a purchase that gives a hit of serotonin.

Toxic spending habit:

....

....

Toxic spending habit:

....

....

Toxic spending habit:

....

....

The thing about credit spending

We'll talk about debt and how to tackle it in more detail a little later on, but it's worth noting here that the way we spend when we're using a credit card or a 'buy now, pay later' service is often different to the way we spend with cash. Paying with credit allows us to delay the effect of our purchase on our financial landscape, enabling us to separate the pleasure of buying from the pain of paying. Not associating the financial cost of something with the item itself can cause problems: it skews our judgement when deciding whether or not something is 'worth it'.

Do you find that you're more willing to pay for 'guilty pleasure' items with a credit card or a 'buy now, pay later' scheme than you would be if you had to part with cash in your bank account? Look back through your credit card statements, and list the kind of things you tend to use credit for.

....

....

....

....

....

....

....

....

....

Why do you think that is?

....

....

....

....

....

....

....

Now, is there anything that you can identify on your statements that you definitely wouldn't have bought if you'd had to pay for it with cash?

....

....

....

....

....

....

....

The emotional spending cycle

Overspending caused by emotional triggers is a very common issue and, although yet to be officially categorised as a form of addiction, the compulsion to shop can be incredibly difficult to resist. Often, the cycle goes like this:

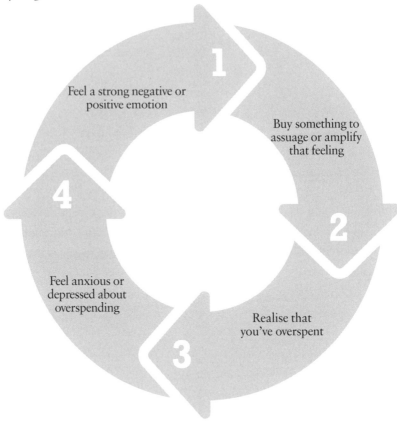

Once begun, this cycle can be difficult to break, and can continue for years on end, creating a spiral of negative feelings around money and a steadily declining confidence in your own ability to manage your cash. Even once identified, it can be easy to laugh off for a time, especially in our current culture of consumerism – but that doesn't negate the very real effect this cycle has on your mental health and financial situation.

Triggers for emotional spending

- boredom
- loneliness
- rejection
- low mood
- anxiety
- jealousy

- FOMO
- work stress
- tiredness
- feeling overwhelmed
- grief

Or, conversely:

- happiness
- confidence

- feeling good, and not wanting to 'ruin' it by thinking of your budget

Think about the things that trigger emotional spending for you. It might help to look back through some bank statements and identify purchases that you made for the wrong reasons, then think about what prompted that behaviour.

....

....

....

....

....

....

....

Breaking the cycle

These emotional forces can override your normal, logical decision-making process, and make it very difficult to know whether you're spending for the right reasons or the wrong ones. I have found that the best way to tackle this problem is to introduce some circuit-breaker questions every time you feel the urge to spend.

It's very difficult to completely overcome the urge to spend emotionally, but in a lot of ways, that doesn't matter – because even if it's hard to get rid of the impulse altogether, what we can change is the way that we deal with that impulse. We don't have to condemn ourselves to a life of overspending and financial anxiety just because we get tempted to hit the shops (or, more realistically, our smartphones) when we're struggling to cope with – or need a distraction from – the way we're feeling. There's no need to perpetuate the self-fulfilling prophecy of being 'bad with money' any longer. We can turn the cycle into a circuit, with switches along the way that can help us put a halt to a sequence of events that can sometimes feel inevitable.

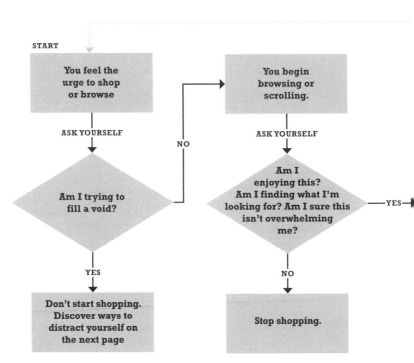

This diagram is something you should be able to come back to time after time, on every occasion where those toxic spending habits start to coax you back again. You can customise it with your own notes, or add more circuit-breaker questions as you figure out what works for you. Once you are able to weed out all of your toxic or impulsive spending habits, you will be able to develop a healthy way of shopping.

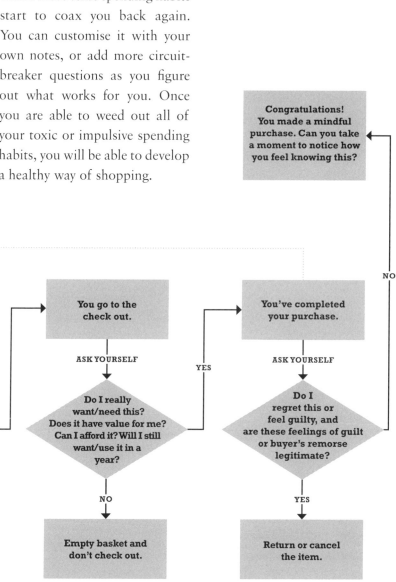

Congratulations! You made a mindful purchase. Can you take a moment to notice how you feel knowing this?

You go to the check out.

ASK YOURSELF

Do I really want/need this? Does it have value for me? Can I afford it? Will I still want/use it in a year?

NO

Empty basket and don't check out.

YES

You've completed your purchase.

ASK YOURSELF

Do I regret this or feel guilty, and are these feelings of guilt or buyer's remorse legitimate?

NO

YES

Return or cancel the item.

A quick checklist for reducing impulse spending

☐ Unsubscribe from marketing emails.

☐ Delete shopping apps.

☐ Remove your credit and debit card details from your device's autofill function.

☐ Disable thumbprint payments on your phone.

☐ Create a rule that you will always sleep on non-essential purchase decisions, and enlist someone to help you to do this.

☐ Have a phone curfew (most people find that their impulse spending happens later in the evening).

What to do instead of spending

Here are some things you could try instead of making a purchase next time you feel the need for a spending fix. Add your own ideas, too.

- **Meditate.**
- **Go out for a walk.**
- **Pick up the phone and call someone for a chat.**
- **Read a book.**
- **Write down how you're feeling.**
- **Listen to a podcast.**
- **Watch a TV show or film that you enjoy (and really *watch* it – don't double-screen).**
- **Do some stretches.**

- **Paint your nails (this is a good one, as you won't be able to operate your phone or computer for at least a few minutes while the polish is drying).**

-

  ....

-

  ....

-

  ....

-

  ....

Separating 'wants' from 'needs' – and planning to afford both

Spending money is not something we can simply opt out of entirely; like food and sleep, it's an important and unavoidable part of life. Instead, we need to find a way to make it work for us.

Before we dive in, I'm going to begin with a bold statement. It's something that seems to have got lost in the (justified) backlash against consumerism and the trends towards minimalism and frantic frugality in some social media spheres.

It's OK to want things.

And I mean material things, holidays, pricey day trips.

As we grow more consumed and distracted by the daily comings and goings of our lives, it can become increasingly difficult to tell what we 'want' and what we 'need'. It's easy to become fixated on certain items that we feel we 'need': things that we tell ourselves will fix everything. It might be a material possession (I'd be able to manage my life much better if I had a Dyson AirWrap) or an experience (we just need a holiday), but usually whatever you are trying to solve comes from somewhere deeper than just flat hair or wanderlust. It's easy to get fixated on certain 'wonder' products and see them as necessities, rather than things that many people manage to live successful and fulfilled lives without. It's easy to fall into the trap of thinking that a certain material possession is the gateway to whatever you want to achieve.

Nine times out of ten, that's not the case. I'm not being flippant about the importance of access to technology, but I wrote my first book on a very old laptop with a damaged screen and a broken charging port, meaning that I could only work for an hour at a time. I'm writing this one on a new MacBook – a much agonised-over investment in my career – and I can tell you honestly, it's been no easier to get the words on to the page. Often, we talk ourselves into thinking that everything will magically fall into place when we finally get 'the thing' – and then we get it, and things don't fall into place. This can leave us with an empty feeling that perpetuates the toxic spending cycle we looked at earlier.

Identifying needs

Since I began my own journey to pull apart and rebuild my relationship with money, I've realised that I actually 'need' very little. I need time and space to work, I need quality time with my family, I need decent food and a roof over my head, and I need adequate storage for my husband's inexplicably large collection of football shirts. Those are the things that I need in order to function and be largely content. The difficulty is that every person has different needs: ones that are completely unique to them. When you are considering a purchase, the best way to tell whether it is a 'want' or a 'need' (if you don't immediately know) is to write the item down, and then wait for a while.

Use the page opposite to keep a running list of things that initially feel like a 'need' to you.

Item	Cost	Date

Once you've added something to the list, wait a week or two and see whether you still feel like you need it, or if you've found a way to make things work without it.

Working out priorities

Of course, just because you need something, doesn't mean that you can necessarily afford it. Use the space below to keep a running list of the things that you need, how much they will cost and how much of a priority they are (ranging from low- to high-priority). I find prioritising really useful, because it helps me to keep my perspective when I'm presented with a Facebook ad for one of the things further down the list (usually straight after a casual chat about said thing with my husband – our phones are definitely listening to us!).

Item	Cost	Priority

What you want

Going back to what I said originally, though: we're allowed to want things. Reducing how much we consume is a great thing – for our bank balances, for our wellbeing and for the environment – but it's quite unrealistic for most people to stop wanting completely. Spending money that you've worked hard to earn on something that you really want can actually be a very rewarding experience, and I can attest to the fact that paying for a considered 'treat' purchase with properly 'disposable' cash rather than credit is an absolute thrill. It took me a while to stop feeling guilty about buying inessential things, because I had managed to get those judgements so wrong in the past, and I needed time to learn to trust myself again when it came to 'unnecessary purchases'. Just as with the 'needs' lists, I have found that keeping a running list of things that I want is super helpful – not only because it helps me to spend mindfully, but also because whenever I'm asked what I want for my birthday or Christmas, I have a ready-made list to refer back to. And if it's not special enough to be a birthday or Christmas gift, then what's it doing on my 'Want List' anyway?

My Want List has a 'Why?' column – not because I think anyone should have to painstakingly justify everything they buy for themselves, but just to make sure that everything on the list is there for the right reasons, and that I'm not going to end up with buyer's remorse afterwards. If the reason something is on your Want List is simply that your favourite influencer has it, or that you've seen it so many times on Instagram that it's now etched on to the backs of your eyelids, then it probably doesn't belong on this list, but in a special filing cabinet we'll be learning about next (the 'I saw it on social media' bin). Start your own Want List here:

Item	Cost	Why?

The 'I saw it on social media' bin

We all know that social media can be a great place to get inspiration for everything from fashion and interiors to careers and creativity, but we also know that it's been increasingly co-opted by big brands wanting to sell to us, whether in paid media ads or via collaborations with creatives and influencers. The effect of this is not only acute (we see a gorgeous dress on a gorgeous person, and we want to own it there and then), but also cumulative (we see a huge number of our 'peers' enjoying lovely lifestyles filled with luxury goods, and our expectations for our own lives, homes and wardrobes are elevated, whether or not we have the means to afford these things). As retailers seek to remove friction from the customer journey by decreasing the number of clicks you need to make to get you from Instagram to the 'Thanks for your order' page, it's becoming easier and easier to sleepwalk your way through social media purchases and then end up footing the bill for something you weren't even properly committed to in the first place. Sometimes, even if you manage to resist this slippery slope, the item remains lodged in your brain – so please feel free to chuck any abandoned impulse social media purchases in the bin opposite. This can include items where you've caught yourself before checking out, and those items you've decided against putting on your Want List after considering the 'why' column.

Ways to afford your Want List

Once you've decided what you want, there's the challenge of affording it. In a lot of cases, creating an allowance in your budget for treat purchases can work really well – you can spend it monthly or allow it to roll over for more expensive things. If your 'want' is quite big and something of a long-term goal, you might want to use the saving tools later on in order to be able to afford it. As an example, I'm currently saving to have a truly awful tattoo removed. Who said your Want List has to be all jade facial rollers and glamping?

In the short term, however, there might be some ways to fund those wants. Here are a few ideas:

Sell something

Not only does this provide you with some extra cash to put towards the things you want, it also extends the lifespan of things you don't want any more, providing someone else with a bargain: win-win.

Consider buying second-hand

There is such a huge market for second-hand products now, as people are choosing not to buy new, both for environmental and money-saving reasons. Even if it's a very specific thing that you want, it's worth checking eBay, Preloved and Facebook Marketplace to see whether you can find it there – you might get lucky, and you'll probably save a fortune.

Check if the retailer has sample sales or refurbished items

Typically, you can find big savings on refurbished or ex-display technology and furniture, but luxury mattress companies also refurbish returns from their trial periods (replacing the outer shell) with massive reductions. We recently bought one for less than a third of the RRP, and it has changed my life.

Collect points

It's not exactly instant gratification, but saving Boots Advantage and Nectar points for a future spree can be really rewarding. I only recently got a Nectar card and have already built up a decent stash of points through my weekly supermarket shops: food accounts for a large part of our monthly expenditure, as it does for most people. I dread to think how many point-collecting opportunities I've missed out on in the last few years, but, as with most good habits, the next best time to start is right now.

Borrow it

I don't know when we all got so obsessed with owning things, but we seem to have lost the sharing instinct as our society moved from a community mindset to an individual one. If you suspect that you might only use an item for a short while, or even just a couple of times, then see if there's a way that you can borrow it. With books, of course, the library (if you still have one) is your go-to resource, while 'sharing shops', where you can borrow everything from drills to tennis rackets for a small daily fee, have recently started to crop up. Rental services for things like children's clothes and toys are also an emerging resource, meaning that you can spread the cost without relying on credit.

Adding value to your possessions beyond the checkout

When a brand slaps a price tag on an item, they are giving it a certain value – but that value isn't fixed. If the item doesn't sell, the price is often slashed in the sale. If the item sells out immediately and is in short or limited supply, the value of it increases massively – think people reselling tickets on StubHub. In the same way, the value that you give to an item once it's in your possession matters. If you buy something and then leave it to gather dust at the back of a cupboard, you're depleting that item's value to nothing. But if you use it every day, if you properly enjoy it, if it makes life easier or more pleasurable for you, you increase its value immeasurably – and there's nothing better than feeling that something you bought was really, really worth it.

Try to think of some items in your home that you are not currently valuing or using. Is there a way you can increase their value by using or treasuring them more?

....

....

....

....

We all make mistakes

The way that we spend is complex and often very deep-rooted. Not only do we often find that our spending patterns are influenced by our emotions, but there are external forces at play, too. Entire industries have grown around the art of making people buy things that they don't need. Our whole economy is built on consumerism, and brands quite simply don't care whether or not you can really afford their product – they just want you to buy it. It's their job to build a customer journey that ushers you through to a purchase as swiftly and seamlessly as possible, and they will play on your emotions as much as they like in order to get you to the end destination. Whole systems are designed to scoop up people who've drifted away from making a purchase and to pour them back into the top of the machine, this time trying a different offer, some different storytelling, a different form of button-pushing. They manipulate our emotions in order to get us to part with our cash, and it can be very, very difficult to resist – so you shouldn't beat yourself up over the odd slip-up. It is not my goal to eliminate impulse purchases from the planet, but to make sure that your spending is mostly mindful, most of the time. Don't let a couple of mistakes ruin your progress. Sometimes it takes the sting out of them to write these mistakes down – and this can also help you identify some of the tactics different retailers use. Do that here, if you want to:

....

....

....

....

It takes time

I really hope that this section has helped you to understand your spending behaviour better, and to perhaps step out of the vortex of emotional spending. Please keep revisiting this chapter every time you feel the pull of an impulse purchase that you can't afford, or if you want to add to one of your lists. Spending habits can take time to change, but eventually spending mindfully becomes second nature.

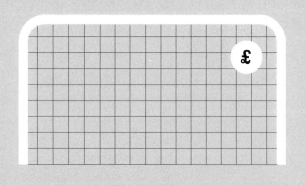

Chapter Five
Setting Goals

Goal-setting is one of the cornerstones of any and every pursuit we might choose to embark on in our lives, and it's important to get it right. If your goals are too ambitious – or not ambitious enough – you might find that your motivation gets snuffed out fairly early in your journey. This section is your space to set goals that lead you to the future that you want for yourself – not just in terms of your financial situation, but in terms of your life as a whole. It's an opportunity to think about what motivates you, and to create a vision for what you'd like your life to be like – something to keep you motivated when the journey feels long and boring (which, sometimes, it will).

When I started out on this journey myself, I didn't have a clear set of goals. I knew that I wanted the debt gone, and that I needed to completely rebuild my relationship with money in order to do that, but I didn't have a clear vision of why, or what came next. It served me fine in the beginning, but when I started to lack motivation and hit a couple of hurdles (three new tyres and a pair of brake discs, to be precise), I recognised the need to pin down what it was that I wanted for my own future, and that of my family. I found that goal-setting in itself was quite intimidating, like being asked what you want to be when you grow up all over again. Sometimes, when you're at a low ebb, it's hard to feel worthy of achieving what you want, and for a long time, the thought of a financially stable future felt way out of my grasp. It existed only in a fantasy world where I won the lottery – it didn't feel achievable at all. Over time, that changed, and I'm now at a point where my bigger financial goals, like buying a house, feel like they might be reachable one day.

Tips for setting achievable goals

I have a long history of setting myself unachievable goals – from weight loss to word counts – as a form of self-punishment, and I do not recommend it. Setting outrageously ambitious goals with overly short deadlines can actually act as a sort of declaration of self-loathing. In setting yourself up to fail, you are actively sabotaging your own efforts before you've even begun (see page 181 for more about self-sabotage). When it comes to achieving your goals, the age-old phrase 'better late than never' springs to mind. It's important to be ambitious, and to feel driven about getting to where you want to be, but make sure that you don't take it too far. If you find you're ahead of your initial goals, you can always set new, more challenging ones.

In the same vein, though, it's important not to make your goals too small or easy, because then they become easily dismissed or postponed. In other words, you need to be the Goldilocks of goal-setters – they need to be just right.

An achievable goal should:

- stretch you gently, but not so far that you snap
- have a timeframe attached, but be flexible –
  because life does get in the way sometimes, and
  we have to adapt
- be specific – having a general vision is good,
  but you need to be able to see a clear path to
  achieving your goal
- be one of few, not many – it's better to have
  three or four goals and achieve them, than have
  ten and forget about them

A vision for your future

This is about the big picture: the life that you want to live and how you want to feel about money in your future. You can be as creative as you like with this, but I want you to fill the following page with words and pictures to give a broad view of how you want things to be. This is something to keep in mind when setting all of your specific long- and short-term goals, because each and every one of them should lead back to this one vision. This vision might change over time as you start to see your hard work come to fruition, and with the natural undulations of life, but the core feeling will probably remain the same.

Having an overarching vision of the future you want is important, because we have a tendency to separate our financial goals from our life goals, choosing arbitrary measures of success that have nothing to do with what will actually make us happy. Establishing this vision will help you to tie your financial journey to your life goals.

My vision

Identifying long-term goals

Once you have an idea of the big picture, it's time to break that down into its component parts and set specific goals that relate to that vision. Is your future happiness based around family? A feeling of home? Travel? Retiring early and having more time with those you love? Learning a new skill or changing career? A combination of all of these?

One of the hardest things about a difficult or precarious financial situation is that it can make you feel trapped: in a job, in a home or even in a relationship that isn't making you happy. For example, my husband's career involves long and antisocial working hours. It means I often turn up to family parties alone with our children, and that we pass like ships in the night for weeks at a time. But, more importantly than that, it means we just spend a lot of time really missing each other. He's very good at his job, but it's a career that he fell into by default in order to support our family when we were faced with an unplanned pregnancy, and the plan has always been for him to have the option to retrain at some point. However, in order to have the freedom and the financial space to create a better family life for ourselves, we need to pay off our debt and build some savings.

We are also one of the many families stuck paying very high rent, which limits our ability to save for a house deposit, even though we could very easily afford a sizeable monthly mortgage. It feels like a catch-22 situation, and one that we'd very much like to escape from as soon as possible. But we also need to significantly reduce our debt in order to redirect our disposable income towards saving for a house deposit, and to make us better candidates for a mortgage. A family home that we own is important to us: it would mean that we'd be unlikely to need to move at short notice, giving us a more stable home for our children (and ourselves); we'd be able to decorate it however we like; and we wouldn't have to ask the landlord's permission to get a pet. In addition, of course, building equity in our own home rather than just paying rent to cover someone else's mortgage has a certain appeal.

With all this in mind, these are our long-term goals:

- **We want to be free of non-mortgage debt and build some savings, creating a stable enough financial position to allow us more time together as a family.**
- **We want to own our own family home.**
- **We want to be able to afford to travel with our children every couple of years.**

These goals are not very big or flashy, but they're what will make us happy. Have a think about your own long-term goals, and write them down below. Try to stick to two or three, and think about how they relate to your big-picture vision.

1.
....

2.
....

3.
....

Short-term goals

Long-term goals are great for envisaging the life that you want and giving yourself something to aim for, but waiting such a long time for the sense of achievement that comes with reaching a goal can be demotivating. Short-term goals give us scope for the little wins that keep us going on what can be a long and sometimes frustrating journey, and pave the way for those bigger targets.

You might choose to set short-term goals on a monthly or weekly basis, and they can be to do with anything – mindset, spending behaviour, saving, paying off debt – it's up to you. In the beginning, one of my short-term goals was to get in touch with my lenders and overcome my anxiety around speaking to finance professionals. I went after that goal over the course of a few weeks, and my confidence in those situations improved far more rapidly than I expected. I thought it was a small goal, but it helped me to lay the foundations for a completely different money mindset. There's space below for three sets of three short-term goals of your own.

1. . . . .

2. . . . .

3. . . . .

1. . . . .

2. . . . .

3. . . . .

1. . . . .

2. . . . .

3. . . . .

All of these little achievements add up over time to something much, much bigger, and they help you to form positive habits, too. Don't be dismissive of little wins, because they are what will carry you through to your bigger goals.

Using money as a tool

Completing these goal-setting exercises makes us think not only about what we want for the future, but also about what's fundamentally important to us now. Fixing your relationship with money is not about making cash the centre of your universe; it's about separating it from your sense of self-worth and, instead, using it as the useful tool that it is.

Think about how you've used money in the past. Have you used it with purpose, or has it just been a footnote in your considerations?

Can you think of a time when you've used money well?

....

....

....

And how about a time when you've misused it?

....

....

....

Think about the difference in how you feel about these two situations. Does one make you feel proud and the other ashamed? What we're looking to eventually achieve is a sort of state of money neutrality, whereby we don't experience these big spikes in emotion in relation to our spending behaviour. Instead, we're aiming for a sense that money is one of the many tools at our disposal as we navigate our way through life, rather than the be-all and end-all.

Dealing with setbacks

It can be tempting to brush any setbacks under the carpet, but it's worth taking a look at what actually happened, so that you can see if there's a way of avoiding the same situation arising again in the future. For example, one of our major setbacks occurred quite early in our journey, when my husband's car needed some work doing in order to pass its MOT. We had been ploughing all of our money into paying off debt, without setting any aside for emergencies. This meant that, when we were faced with a large, unexpected bill, we had to use one of our credit cards to pay for it, temporarily increasing our debt and leaving us feeling like we'd taken a massive step backwards. In order to avoid a setback like this in the future, we quickly realised that, alongside paying off our debt as efficiently as possible, we also needed to maintain a small pot of savings for situations such as this.

Use the space below to document any setbacks that happen to you. Write down how you feel about them, and what you might be able to do differently to either prevent them from happening again, or to stop them from having such a negative impact.

....

....

....

....

....

....

....

Holding yourself accountable

The promises that we make to ourselves are often the hardest ones to keep, especially when we're feeling down on ourselves. Prioritising your own long-term wellbeing and continuing to work on it every day isn't easy. You might not feel deserving of the time and effort required to push through the more difficult days, or you might simply feel that letting yourself down isn't as much of a big deal as letting others down.

As I've mentioned before, the line between accountability and self-punishment can be quite a blurry one. It's important to address any slip-ups you might have, and to pick up on waning motivation before it becomes an issue, but it's also good to remember that nobody's perfect, and that you won't get everything absolutely right first time. The vital thing is to keep going, and to keep your eyes on the prize.

Tips for holding yourself accountable

- **Revisit your goals frequently.**
- **Have an 'accountability buddy' – someone you trust, who will check in with you.**
- **Measure your progress in a way that motivates you.**
- **Set small rewards for goals achieved.**

Progress isn't linear

Often, when we embark on a journey to try and improve something about our lives, we set out with the unrealistic expectation that a graph of our progress will look like this:

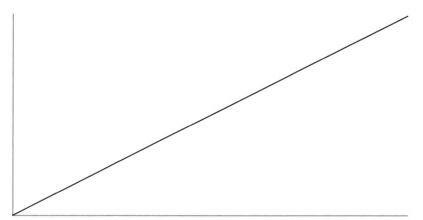

When actually, it almost always looks like this:

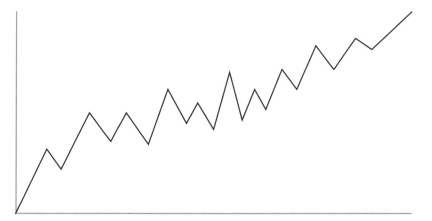

The key is to look at the overall trend – as long as it's generally going upwards, you're doing well. Focus on the progress, learn from the setbacks and use any periods where you feel like you're plateauing or treading water to reflect on what needs to happen to propel you forwards.

Use the axes below to plot a graph of your progress throughout your time using this journal – it could be towards a specific goal or just towards that big-picture vision that you set out at the beginning of this section.

Progress towards goal

Time

Remember your goals

Revisit this section often to stay in touch with your goals, and to keep the reasons why you're doing this at the forefront of your mind: this is going to be crucial to your success. There will always be days where it all feels a bit pointless, and you feel like giving up. By coming back here, you'll remind yourself of the goals that you've achieved so far, and of where it is that you want to end up.

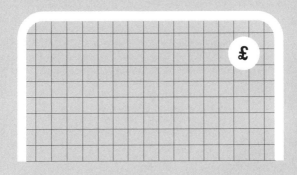

'By coming back here, you'll remind yourself of the goals that you've achieved so far, and of where it is that you want to end up.'

Chapter Six
Paying Off Debt

Although debt is only one of a plethora of different symptoms of a difficult relationship with money, it can be one of the more stressful and anxiety-inducing ones. I know, first-hand, that debt can feel like a huge chasm between you and the life that you want to be living, which is why it's a priority to tackle debt as part of this process. In fact, for me, the bulk of this journey so far has been about paying off debt. With such a significant amount of it weighing on my shoulders, and incurring so much interest as time went by, the best decision for both my mental and financial health was to concentrate on clearing it, in order to be able to see the wood for the trees.

Not all debt is made equal, though. A small balance on a 0% interest credit card does not usually come with the same emotional burden and sense of urgency as a large balance spread across several, interest-incurring cards, and it might be that your priorities are slightly different from mine. Use this chapter (and the next, which is about saving) according to your own needs and priorities.

Adding it all up

Opening up all your statements or apps and getting an idea of the lay of the land can be quite a scary and emotional process, so do this in your own time. For some people, the right approach is to rip the plaster off and get it over with, and for others this is best done gradually. List all of your credit cards and accounts, including overdrafts, loans, store cards and 'buy now, pay later' accounts, in the table below, making sure you include all of the key information.

Credit card/account	Starting balance	Interest rate

Dealing with the emotions attached to your debt

If only it were as simple as just adding up the numbers. When I finally bit the bullet and looked at the sum total of the debts that I'd accrued over the previous few years, I remember it felt like it was going to consume me. I couldn't see how I'd allowed things to get to that point, and I just felt completely bathed in shame and anger with myself.

You might be feeling a complicated mixture of things, and seeing a final figure in black and white can feel quite overwhelming. Use this space to write down how you're feeling about it all.

....

....

....

....

....

....

....

....

....

Often, it's not even really about the actual amount of debt – after all, we all have different incomes and assets, so what feels like a small amount to one person might feel like a colossal amount to another. Never forget that this is about your own personal journey, and neither I nor anyone else can tell you how to feel about any of this. So much of personal finance is entirely subjective – and that includes the use of debt and credit.

Often, the shame we feel around debt comes from a sense of having lost control. You might feel that the money was wasted, or that you've got nothing to show for it, or that what you do have to show for it wasn't worth it. Trust me when I say that everyone makes mistakes like this in their life, whether the cost is monetary, or comes in the form of some other sacrifice, such as health or time.

The moralising of debt and money worries within societal narratives is something that can have a huge impact on how we feel about our own financial situations and, in turn, our feelings of self-worth. Often, particularly in fictional representations of financial difficulty, debt is portrayed as a sign of weakness of character – think Becky Bloomwood, Carrie Bradshaw or even Ted Hastings from *Line of Duty*. Their financial difficulties were always shown to be either a result of frivolous and materialistic behaviour, or something that made them less trustworthy – or both. This kind of thing can seep into our consciousness and cause us to start feeling these things about ourselves, too. For a very long time, I would wince every time I saw debt mentioned in this way. Whenever I saw an article about how someone – invariably a woman – had put thousands of pounds' worth of cosmetic surgery on a credit card, I would think of my own bank balance and feel ashamed. But as I've progressed in my personal journey and heard more from those in similar situations, I've come to realise that there is a nuance to debt that just doesn't exist in mainstream coverage of financial difficulty. Like everything else in life, it's a complex issue with a vast array of causes and effects, and it requires quite a lot of unpicking in order to be fully understood.

Hopefully, some of the earlier work that we've done in this journal has given you the tools to start working through these feelings, to open up to someone you trust and to seek the help that you need, if you need it. The negative feelings will start to subside as you come to terms with your debt and start to pay it back – I promise.

Language tip: Stop saying 'I'm in debt'; start saying 'I have debt'

It's just a small tweak in the way that we speak about our financial situations, but switching 'I'm in debt' to 'I have debt' helps us to distance what we owe from our feelings of self-worth. The former conjures up the image of being stuck at the bottom of a deep pit, which is sometimes what debt can feel like, but that kind of all-consuming hopelessness isn't helpful. By saying 'I have debt', we claim the debt as our own, taking responsibility for it, but we don't absorb it into our sense of self. Using this shift in perception, we can start to see our debt as a problem that we need to solve, rather than a part of ourselves that we hate.

Can you save yourself interest with a transfer?

If you're paying interest on your credit card balance and your credit score is OK, it's worth checking to see whether or not you're eligible for a 0% balance transfer. This involves applying for a new credit card and transferring the balance of your existing card, so that you're no longer being charged interest on the amount. It can incur a small fee, and sometimes you won't know the card limit or the length of your interest-free period until you've been accepted, but it can be a really efficient way to pay off your debt more quickly.

If you go for one of these transfers, the key is to make sure that you remain committed to paying off the debt, and also to ensure you clear as much as possible within the interest-free period, because these types of cards usually jump right up to a high interest rate after the offer ends.

For more information on balance transfers, check out moneysavingexpert.com. They have a tool for checking your eligibility without affecting your credit rating, which can be really helpful – just make sure that you're using it for the right reasons, and not to score more interest-free credit that might come back to haunt you later.

Methods for paying off debt

Although paying off debt and taking control of your finances can be a bit of a process of trial and error, and needs to be tailored to suit your individual character and lifestyle, there are certain methods that can help to give a sense of structure to your plan. Below are descriptions of three different methods that you might use, with pros and cons for each. Give them all a read before you decide which one is right for you.

Highest interest first

This method makes the most objective financial sense: by paying off the debts incurring the highest percentage of interest first, you save yourself money in the long run. This is also known as the 'avalanche' method.

For this method, you list all of your debts from highest interest to lowest, then repay as much as you can afford on the highest-interest card or credit account, while making minimum repayments on the rest. Once the highest-interest debt is paid off in full, you move on to the second highest-interest card or account on the list, adding the repayment amount you were making on the first card to the minimum amount you were already paying on the second. Continue in this way until all of your debt is cleared.

Pros:
- It minimises the amount of interest you'll pay overall.
- It makes the most logical sense.

Cons:
- It might take a while to clear your first debt, especially if your highest-interest account also has the biggest balance to pay off.
- Waiting a long time for a 'win' can have an impact on your motivation overall.

Lowest balance first

Although not necessarily the quickest way to pay off your debt, this method is popular because it allows you to go for the 'quick wins' first. While you will end up paying more interest overall, you might be more likely to stick with paying off your debt because you're motivated by hitting those early goals. You might have also seen this referred to as the 'snowball' method.

For this method, you list all of your debts from lowest balance to highest, then repay as much as you can afford on the lowest balance on the list, while making minimum repayments on the rest, until your lowest balance is paid off in full. You then move on to the next lowest balance on the list, adding the repayment amount you were making on the first balance to the minimum amount you were already paying on the second. Continue in this way until all of your debt is cleared.

Pros:
- **Wins early on are good for motivation.**
- **You'll reduce your overall number of debts faster.**

Cons:
- **You'll pay more interest overall.**
- **You're saving your biggest debts for last, which might hinder motivation later on.**

Fixed payments

This one pretty much does what it says on the tin. You make set payments towards each of your debts, each one of them over the minimum repayment amount. I found that this method worked for me in the beginning, as I was particularly anxious about my debt and wanted to make progress on each of my cards.

For this method, list all of your debts in any order and split your repayment budget out according to what makes sense to you. As individual debts are paid off, you redistribute that repayment amount out amongst your remaining debts.

Pros:
- **No reminders from your lender about making more than the minimum repayment.**
- **A good middle ground if you can't decide on one of the methods above.**

Cons:
- **You'll pay more interest than you would using the 'highest interest first' method.**
- **It might take longer to pay off your first debt than with the 'lowest balance first' method.**

Choosing the right method for you

Hopefully, the previous sections in this journal have helped you to understand a little more about your own money habits and what works for you (and what doesn't) when it comes to your mindset. How you choose to pay off your debt is personal to you, and needs to work for you. Consider where you've slipped up before, especially if you've tried to tackle this in the past without success, and think about what you want to be different this time. Once you've settled on an option, write it here:

I'm using the .... method to clear my debt so that I can move on to a better financial future.

This is the right method for me because:

....

....

....

....

....

....

....

....

....

....

....

....

In the end, it really doesn't matter which method you choose, as long as it's one that you can see yourself sticking with for the duration. Different people will have different ideas about what's best, but a large part of creating your own bespoke financial plan is learning to drown out some of the noise that comes from other people's opinions. It's your own judgement that matters here – trust yourself.

Tracking your progress

In terms of motivation, tracking your progress towards paying off your debt is really important. There's something immensely satisfying about reaching a new milestone, and the process starts to feel like you're moving towards something positive as opposed to running away from something negative. You can use the chart below to track your progress for the next twelve months – it's up to you whether you record your total at the beginning or the end of the month, just make sure you're consistent.

Month	Total debt	Debt paid off this month

Progress grid

While it's definitely satisfying seeing the numbers reduce in a table form, it can help to have a more visual representation of your progress. In order to track my own journey, I use a simple 10 x 10 grid, with each little square representing 1% of my total debt (for example, if your starting debt were £10,000, each square would represent £100). Every month, I colour in the amount of squares that represent the reduction in my debt for that period. If you're a visual person, this kind of tool might work for you, too.

1 square = £_____

Give it a try: there's something about the ritual of colouring in those squares that's very satisfying! Just imagine how great it's going to feel colouring in that very last square.

Celebrate

I'd also really like to give you something to come back to – a declaration of sorts. Once you've cleared your debt, fill this page with a huge celebration. You could write 'I'm debt free!' or 'I'm net positive' in big letters, or you could just scribble a massive explosion of joyous colour. However you feel, get it down. I want you to acknowledge this massive achievement, and take the space you need to celebrate it properly – because you've done something really, really amazing.

Keep going

Coming to terms with your debt and making a plan to pay it off can be one of the biggest roadblocks on the path to taking control of your money, so well done if you've made it here. As someone who's still in the middle of this part myself, I know how slow-going it can seem at times. Sometimes you just have to remember one thing: the time will pass anyway. So you can wake up in a year with this debt still weighing heavily on you, or with it feeling considerably lighter.

'Once you've cleared your debt, fill this page with a huge celebration. You could write "I'm debt free!" or "I'm net positive!" in big letters, or you could just scribble a massive explosion of joyous colour.'

Chapter Seven
Building Some Savings

When you're used to living in a financially precarious position from month to month, or putting big purchases on credit and then 'reverse saving' for them, the idea of having a safety net of cash stashed away might feel completely alien to you. For a long time, I struggled to save. As my debt grew, I felt torn between my desire to pay into my savings account and the necessity of making my repayments. I would often make deposits into an ISA only to need the money a week later, a cycle of behaviour that made me lose confidence and feel like I was treading water. None of this was conducive to a healthy relationship with money, and it felt increasingly like I was never going to be able to build up any savings.

As I started to look at my behaviour with money and the many ways in which it was counterproductive, I realised that my saving behaviour was just as damaging as my spending behaviour. I was discouraging myself by being too ambitious, and my savings goals were big, but not very specific. I would set abstract timeframes, but not really look at how much I needed to be saving each month in order to hit that goal. So, I decided to start small, making paying off my debt a priority (see chapter 6 for more on this), but also making incremental savings deposits in order to slowly build up a backup fund.

How do you feel about your current savings situation?

....

....

....

....

Why saving is important

It took me a while to understand the importance of having savings, but the benefits of investing some of your income in your future are myriad. First and foremost, savings act as a financial parachute – something to fall back on when things get tough, or when unforeseen circumstances arise. As a family, we have seen our fair share of job losses, reductions in income and unexpected bills, and never had the peace of mind that comes with knowing you can cover your expenses for a month or two while you straighten things out. For us, credit and asking family for help were our only options, and neither of those is ideal. Keeping an 'emergency fund' that will cover you if the rug gets pulled out from under you will benefit you both financially and psychologically – not only when the chips are down, but in the meantime, too. It's a feeling of security that enables you to feel more in control of your life.

As well as the security element of having savings, taking the time to save up for the things you want is immensely satisfying. As someone who relied on credit for big purchases for a long time, the thrill (and delayed gratification) of buying a new computer with money that I'd actually saved up first was wonderful. Saving for a purchase gives us the time we need to be sure about it, and it helps us to really appreciate the value of the item we're buying.

In a more abstract sense, saving gives us the feeling of building something positive, and it also buys us freedom – the freedom to take risks, to work less, or maybe even to retire early. Building up a big enough financial cushion means that we are more in control of our own destiny, rather than having our future dictated to us by our bank balance. By saving, we liberate ourselves from the financial precariousness of living payday to payday.

Think about the reasons why developing better saving habits is important to you. What do you want to get out of saving?

....

....

....

....

....

If you've always wanted to save, but struggled – like many people, myself included – what's been stopping you?

....

....

....

....

Saving methods and tools

As you probably know by now, the least effective way to save is to just wait and see what's left at the end of the month and then transfer it into a savings account, because, unless you're on a very large income, it's too easy for that 'leftover' cash to diminish on incidental expenses without you even really noticing. This approach can also lead you to believe that you just don't earn enough to be able to save anything, which is a problem in itself. Of course, this genuinely is the case for a lot of people, but most of us can afford to set some money aside on a regular basis, even if it's just a very small amount.

Different saving methods work better for different people, depending on what they're saving for, how much they're managing to put away and what their relationship with money is like. Here are a few approaches to consider.

• **For larger, regular amounts,** set up a standing order to your savings account on the day you get paid. Sometimes referred to as 'paying yourself first', this method means that the money you've budgeted for saving leaves your current account almost as soon as it's landed. If you want to spend it, you'll have to withdraw it from your savings, which adds an extra bit of friction to the purchase process and forces you to consider whether or not you actually want the thing. With this approach, it's best to set up your arrangement for a more modest amount to begin with, so that you don't leave yourself short for bills.

• **For smaller amounts,** rounding-up or 'save the change' tools can be a great way to save without noticing much of a change throughout the month. Some banks offer this option within your current account, or you can use an app like Moneybox to save or invest the change that you would receive from things like a cup of coffee or a couple of hours' parking. Similarly, using a savings app like Chip or Plum, where small amounts of your balance are siphoned off every few days according to an affordability algorithm, can help to get you into the saving habit if it's something that you've always found difficult. See pages 139–140 for more on these tools.

- **Savings 'challenges'** are a great way to make saving fun. These are often built in as triggers in savings apps, but you can do them manually, too.

Could a savings challenge help you to reach your goals?

If you're saving for something huge, like a house deposit or pension, the small amounts put aside in these challenges might offer a contribution, but are unlikely to get you there on their own. However, if what you're looking to do is build up a cushion, have a bit of cash to splash on yourself, or save for expensive occasions like Christmas, birthdays or weddings, savings challenges can be a great method to use. Here are a few examples of different savings challenges.

The rainy day challenge

This involves transferring a small amount of money to your savings every time it rains. If you live in the UK, this could end up being quite lucrative!

The penny-saving challenge

This challenge allows you to save £667.95 in one year, starting with just 1p. It's quite a manual challenge, as it involves transferring a daily amount to your savings, but this might not be such a bad thing for many of us, as it forces you to check your bank balance. The amounts are so small – starting with a penny and then increasing by 1p each day until you reach £3.65 at the end of the year – but the amount you end up saving would probably be enough to cover all of your Christmas presents.

The 52-week challenge

Here, you put away an increasing amount each week. Start with £1 the first week, then £2 the second week, and so on. By the end of the year-long challenge, you will have £1,378 in savings. You can also do this in reverse, starting with £52.

If you'd like to try out the 52-week challenge, you can use this section to track your progress – just colour in each coin as you transfer the money into your savings account. I find it easiest to set a specific day for the transfer, perhaps on a Sunday evening, or whenever else you want to do your weekly money audit (see page 162 for more on this). You could also create something similar yourself for the penny challenge.

£1 £2 £3 £4 £5 £6 £7

£8 £9 £10 £11 £12 £13 £14

£15 £16 £17 £18 £19 £20 £21

£22 £23 £24 £25 £26 £27 £28

£29 £30 £31 £32 £33 £34 £35

£36 £37 £38 £39 £40 £41 £42

£43 £44 £45 £46 £47 £48 £49

£50 £51 £52

Tools and apps to help you

If you already have enough to remember, or are dealing with too many daily or weekly tasks as it is – as many of us are in this hectic modern life – and you're looking for a way to automate your savings, there are a plethora of helpful tools to make things easier for you. The fintech (financial technology) industry is booming, and is forcing traditional banks to think outside the box and challenge themselves to offer better digital services to their customers. Here are a few tools and apps to help you to save without any effort.

Save the Change

This service is exclusive to Lloyds Banking Group (Lloyds Bank, Halifax and Bank of Scotland). It rounds up every debit card purchase you make to the nearest pound, and automatically transfers the difference to your savings account. So, for example, if you buy something for £2.25, it will round it up to £3 and deposit the 75p in your savings account.

Coin Jar

Exclusive to app-based bank Monzo, this works in a similar way to Save the Change, rounding up your purchases and transferring the difference to a nominated savings pot.

Plum

Plum is a saving and investing app that connects to your bank account via Open Banking. It transfers small amounts every few days according to what its algorithm thinks you can afford. You can tweak the settings depending on how ambitious you want to be, and you can also create pots with targets, add money manually and automate savings challenges. The basic version is free, with options to upgrade.

Chip

Working in a similar way to Plum, Chip siphons off small amounts of money to build savings gradually. You can also adapt the settings to be more or less ambitious, automate payday savings and see when you're on an unbroken saving streak. You can also skip, reduce or increase your autosaves, meaning that you're in complete control if a financial anomaly arises. The basic version is free, with options to upgrade.

Moneybox

Moneybox is another saving and investing app, with more options for those looking to invest money or save into a Lifetime ISA (see below for more types of savings accounts). It has the round-up feature, too. The basic version is free, with options to upgrade.

Types of savings accounts

The type of savings account that you use should depend on what you're using it for, and whether the savings that you're looking to build are for short-term or long-term use. Here's a basic overview of the types of account you can have.

'Pots' or instant access savings

Cash ISAs, online banking 'pots' and app-based savings accounts usually fit into this category. You can access your money immediately with no penalty charge, but the interest is either very low or non-existent. The maximum amount that you can pay into any kind of ISA in one year is £20,000. They're good for emergency funds and money set aside for birthdays, Christmas, etc.

Fixed-term accounts

The interest on these accounts tends to be higher, but you can't withdraw for a fixed period without sacrificing the interest you've earned or even a percentage of your capital. Better for bigger, more future-based savings goals.

Investment accounts

The world of investing is vast, and there's not space to go into it fully here, but an accessible way to invest your money is with a Stocks and

Shares ISA. This is more of a long-term venture, as your capital is at risk. A good place to start learning about this subject is Emilie Bellet's brilliant Vestpod platform.

Lifetime ISA

Lifetime ISAs come in the cash variety and the stocks-and-shares variety, but with an added 25% bonus top-up from the government of up to £1,000 per year. **They can only be used to save for pensions and house deposits**, with a hefty penalty if you withdraw cash for any other reason.

When deciding on the right account for your savings, think about what you're going to be using the money for, and whether or not you might need instant access. It's a good idea to save paying into an investment or Lifetime ISA for after you have an adequate emergency fund set aside.

Saving alongside debt

I recently asked my Instagram followers whether they save alongside paying off debt, and 58% of people who responded said that they do. I was somewhat intrigued and encouraged by this, because much of the advice out there is to refrain from saving and instead pay the maximum off your debt, but it seems that others, like me, see the value in having a safety net. If your debt is interest-free or has a fixed term (like a loan) with an early repayment penalty, it's much easier to decide to save. If you have debt that's incurring a large amount of interest, though, it can feel counter-intuitive not to use every last penny of your income after bills to pay off your debt. However, there are some reasons why saving at least a small amount alongside paying off your debt is something to consider.

• If you channel everything you've got into reducing debt and rely on the 'cushion' in your credit limit for emergencies, it can be really demoralising if you then have to use this cushion and sink further down towards your credit limit, undoing your progress. It feels like a step backwards in a way that using emergency-fund savings doesn't (because that's what they're there for).

- There is a risk that, if you pay everything towards debt and rely on it for a contingency fund, your lender might decide to reduce your credit limit following a change in your credit score or affordability, leaving you high and dry if something unexpected does arise. If the money is in a separate savings account, though, that can't happen.

- If you are struggling to get out of your overdraft and shift your mindset to exclude it from your ideas around what you have available to spend, saving up in a separate account and paying it off in chunks can be easier than trying to reduce it in other ways.

- Lastly, saving is doing something constructive with money. It's building something positive as opposed to just trying to diminish something negative. If your relationship with money has been largely destructive, this can feel like a huge boost and really help with building a positive mindset.

How do you feel about saving alongside debt?

....

....

....

....

How do you think saving might be able to help you to overcome any financial difficulties you might be having?

....

....

....

....

What are you saving for?

One of the things that really helps with the motivation to save is having a clear idea of what you're saving for. Simply transferring an arbitrary amount of money over to a different account each month for the sake of watching it grow might give you a nice, satisfied feeling every now and then, but often that's not enough to encourage a sustained commitment to saving. Instead, giving your money a purpose can push you to prioritise saving over spending, and the satisfaction when you hit your savings goals is huge.

One of the best ways to do this is to look at the cost of the purchase you want to make – be it a car, holiday, house deposit, anything – and the date by which you need to/would like to have it saved. Then divide the amount by how many months (or weeks, if you're paid weekly) there are between now and then, and that gives you the amount that you need to save each week or month in order to get there, making it easier to see whether or not your goal is achievable, and what you might need to sacrifice in order to meet your target.

Take some time to think about what you'd like to save for. It could be a near-future goal or a long-term goal, but it pays to be specific about amounts and timings. Go back to the goal-setting section if you need a little inspiration for this. You can set these targets all at once or one after the other, depending on whether you want to focus on one goal at a time or put your money towards several different targets: it's up to you.

Savings goal one

Goal: ....

....

Savings deadline: ....

Monthly savings amount: ....

Savings goal two

Goal: ....

....

Savings deadline: ....

Monthly savings amount: ....

Savings goal three

Goal: ....

....

Savings deadline: ....

Monthly savings amount: ....

Savings goal four

Goal: ....

....

Savings deadline: ....

Monthly savings amount: ....

Even long after you've completed this journal, setting savings targets is a lifetime habit that's worth getting into. Every time you set a new goal or plan a big purchase, you can use this method to make sure you have the right amount of cash available at the right time.

Tracking your progress

As with paying off debt, if you have a very ambitious savings target – for instance, a house deposit worth tens of thousands of pounds – it can feel like a long slog to get there. Tracking your progress in a visual way can help you to stay motivated and encouraged, and give you a little element of celebration and ceremony in the monthly process of saving.

You can use the grids in this section in a similar way to the one in chapter 6, tracking each contribution towards your savings goal by colouring in a square. To use them, simply divide your target savings amount by 100 to find 1% (so, if you want to save £8,000, 1% is £80) and then colour in a square each time you've deposited that amount in your savings account. There's one big square, for tracking your progress towards a big goal, and three smaller squares, for some of your more short-term savings targets.

Savings goal:

....

....

Total target amount:

....

1% =

....

Savings goal:

🖊

....

....

Total target amount:

🖊

....

1% =

....

Savings goal:

....

....

Total target amount:

....

1% =

....

Savings goal:

🖊️
....

....

Total target amount:

🖊️
....

1% =

🖊️
....

Saving is a positive step

Saving is something that's often as fraught with emotion as debt. We feel ashamed when we don't get it right, and we can sometimes feel like we're treading water even when we have the best of intentions. I hope this section has equipped you with some practical ways to make saving a priority, as well as some tips and tools to motivate you as you start building something positive with your money.

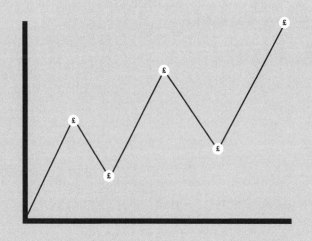

Chapter Eight
Making and Tracking Your Budget

Here it is. The 'B' word. The one that almost everyone still associates with restriction and boredom; the least sexy term in our money vocabulary. Your budget, though, is the thing that ties together all of the elements that we've covered so far. It's your Magna Carta, your big plan for your financial life – and you can't do any of this without it. This section covers all of the things you need to consider when making your budget, how to build one that works for you, and how to keep it up.

Live 'with' a budget, not 'on' one

One small shift in language, one giant leap in mindset. Lots of people might choose to describe themselves as 'on' a budget in the same way that they might describe themselves as being 'on' a diet – a short-term plan with a fixed desired outcome, misery and deprivation not optional. That's not the way to think about budgets.

All your budget is, when it comes right down to it, is a plan for your money. It tells you what's coming in, what's going out, what's left over and what you're going to do with it. None of that information is ever going to stop being relevant during the course of your life – it might be that, when you're more comfortable financially, your plan for what to do with your disposable income changes and relaxes, but it's still something that you should know about. A budget is just your window into what's going on in your bank account and your way to exercise control over the financial outcomes of that, so living with one shouldn't be a temporary or one-time thing.

I've tried to live life 'on' a budget a number of times in the past, and it hasn't worked for me – in the same way that no prescriptive diet has ever worked for me. Think about how the word 'budget' makes you feel. Have you tried and failed to budget in the past? Can you think about why that might have been?

....

....

....

....

....

....

Now, imagine yourself living *with* a budget, in control of your money for the first time in a long time (or maybe ever). How do you think that would feel?

....

....

....

....

....

....

....

Don't crash-budget

I didn't start this journey being friends with my budget. I saw it as a boring, restrictive necessity: a way to whip myself into shape and punish myself for overspending in the past. In the beginning, I pulled the strings as tight as they would go, allowing no wiggle room, no money allocated for enjoyment. But I quickly realised that speed of progress isn't the only thing that matters – longevity and sustainability are important, too. Stripping out every little luxury and leaving yourself with a bare-bones budget might be bearable for a couple of months, but if your goals are further away, a more likely scenario is that you'll begin to flag when your initial burst of motivation burns out. You may grow bitter and resentful of the impact that living with a restrictive budget is having on your life, and ultimately, you might give up. You'll probably return to your old way of doing things, leaving you right back where you started, but with even less faith in yourself.

I understand the allure of a crash budget, of course. Life seems simpler when we polarise our behaviour, and the temptation to inflict something punitive on ourselves when we're angry or disappointed with our past behaviour is completely understandable. It's just that it doesn't tend to work very well, and even if it does, my general feeling is that life's too short to spend a couple of years being completely miserable for any reason. The end doesn't justify the means.

Identifying little luxuries

As a first step towards building your budget, take some time to think about a few things – little luxuries outside of your absolute essential outgoings, that hold real value for you. Things that you would really miss if you gave them up. Then write them below.

....

....

....

....

....

....

....

These are your protected 'frills', the things that will keep you going. Try to find space for them in your budget as you work through this section. We're in this for the long-haul, after all.

Planning a budget that works for you

My budgeting method is not revolutionary. There's no silver bullet that suddenly opens up masses of breathing space between your income and your outgoings. What this section does provide, though, is a basic structure which you can personalise and tailor to suit your specific circumstances and requirements, or those of your household.

Before we lay everything out, it's a good idea to make a note of the different elements that make up your budget. We'll do that now.

Income

If you're salaried, your income will be fixed from month to month (or week to week), while if you're freelance, it might vary. If you have a variable income, work out your budget using the minimum your income could be. I've allowed space for more than one income to make this workable for family finances, but it works fine for one person, too.

Income source	Income amount
Total income:	

Fixed outgoings

Your fixed outgoings are the things that stay the same every month, like your rent or mortgage, council tax, etc. List them below.

Fixed outgoing	Outgoing amount
Total fixed outgoings:	

Variable outgoings

Variable outgoings are those tricksy things that can sometimes completely throw you off – like childcare, debt repayments, petrol and food shopping. List them below, using an honest range for how much they usually cost. We will use the top end of the range in your budget.

Variable outgoing	Outgoing amount
Total variable outgoings:	

Total outgoings (fixed and variable): . . . .

Important!

If your total outgoings exceed your income, and there's nothing left to cut, you need to get in touch with a service for people dealing with financial difficulty (see page 54 for more information). This is a situation that no amount of careful budgeting can solve, but there are services and experts who can help you free of charge.

Disposable income

Remember: be honest, and be accurate.

A lot of my past budgeting failures were down to being vague about figures and omitting certain expenses from my budget. A bit like baking, budgeting requires precision if it's going to work properly, so you need to make a commitment to being accurate and using real figures, as well as being honest about including all your expenses in your budget, even when you're not necessarily proud of the expenditure. Being hazy about your budget might lull you into a false sense of security about how things are going, and can leave you with a nasty shock when you run out of money before the end of the month.

Identifying your budgeting challenges

When it comes to living with a budget, we each have unique challenges and financial blind spots that are just waiting to trip us up – expenses that sort of pass us by, things that we don't factor in. It's helpful to weed these out at this stage so that we can be vigilant and look out for them. They are usually things like incidental purchases, top-up food shops and gifts for other people.

Look back through your bank statements from the last few months, and see if there's anything in there that takes you by surprise – times where you've sort of 'sleep-spent'. Is there a common theme to these purchases? Use the space below to work through this.

....

....

....

....

....

....

Now, make a list of the things you need to keep an eye out for when tracking your expenses: things you might not have considered including when you listed your variable outgoings previously, but that actually do have an impact.

....

....

....

....

All of this might seem a little pedantic if you're used to taking a more broad-brush approach to your finances, as I was, but the small things really do add up, and they can be budget-breaking.

Tools to help you stick to your budget

As with everything, if there's a way to make sticking to your budget easier, it's worth giving it a go. Here are a few additional tools to make running with all this much simpler:

Meal planning

Time and time again, I hear that food is one of the biggest expenditures for households, and one of the most difficult to trim. According to the UK government website, the average expenditure on food for families is 10.6% of the household's total income. This increases to 15.2% of the household's total income for those families whose income is in the UK's lowest 20%. Food costs account for a huge proportion of our outgoings, and yet we often underestimate them, which is easily done if you're in the habit of just popping out for bits and pieces.

Meal planning is a great way to reduce not only what you spend, but what you waste, too. Since we switched to a more organised way of feeding our family, we've been able to drastically reduce the amount of food we don't use, which is good for both our budget and the planet.

Something that I really urge you to do, though, when planning out your weekly meals, is to be realistic. If you find you barely have any time as it is, you're not suddenly going to magic up an extra couple of hours to cook delicious, budget-friendly meals from scratch every single night. Make sure you plan for some easy wins and perhaps the odd meal out or takeaway, because if you're overambitious in your meal plans, you can really trip yourself up. Budgeting for eating out or ordering in is far better than not budgeting for it, then making an exhausted, impromptu order for tikka masala as your fresh ingredients go off in the fridge.

Use the page opposite as a template to plan your meals, or create your own to suit your family.

	Lunch	Dinner
Mon		
Tue		
Wed		
Thu		
Fri		
Sat		
Sun		

Snack ideas for the week: ....

....

Tips for making a meal plan that works and is cost-effective:

- Make a 'capsule fridge', i.e. coordinate meals so that they have one or more ingredient(s) in common – though not so much that you get sick of said ingredient.

- If batch-cooking doesn't work for you (it doesn't for me – I've tried and failed many times), just try to make one extra portion of dishes that keep and reheat well, like chilli and other one-pot dishes, and include repeats in your meal plan.

- Remember that it doesn't have to be fancy to be nutritious. Simple, low-effort dishes can be the backbone of your plan.

- Plan your meals before you go food shopping, and make your shopping list based on your plan.

- Split your weekly shop in two to reduce top-up shops for fresh ingredients.

Make it a ritual

There's absolutely nothing that says that making and tracking your budget has to be a chore. This might sound crazy, but there are actually ways that you can make it something to look forward to. Hopefully, by now, your mindset has shifted to allow you to be open to the idea of looking after your personal finances as a form of looking after yourself, so why not incorporate your money admin with other forms of self-care?

Taking some time to yourself to look over your budget and plan for the month or week ahead can be a really nice thing. I like to do it on a Sunday evening, because it gives me a sense of being prepared for the week, and reduces the Sunday night dread and anxiety that often creeps up on us. Reclaiming this activity as something positive is also important for me, because Sunday nights used to be the time when I would lie awake, worrying about the direct debits that were due to come out the following day, wishing that the weekend reprieve would last a bit longer.

On pages 188–211 you will find weekly journal pages which you can use as a template for these regular financial self-care sessions. Incorporating the act of tracking your budget into your weekly self-care routine will have myriad benefits: so take an hour at a time that suits you, put on some music and use the self-care tips from a few chapters ago to build a ritual for yourself. Fill the following boxes with words and doodles to depict the elements of your weekly or monthly personal finance and self-care ritual – be as creative as you like.

Your monthly budget

Living with a budget is a long-term venture, but in order to get on the right track, it can be helpful to have some structure while you're building positive habits. This next section is for you to apply everything you've learned and to look at the progress that you've made. We begin with three monthly budget spreads to track your income and outgoings. Try to make a habit of planning your budget for each month at the end of the previous month, so that you feel prepared – and remember to check in on a weekly basis, too. On pages 188–211 you will find weekly progress pages; I recommend using these alongside your monthly budgets to keep track of how things are going for you.

It's usually easiest to track your budget over a calendar month, so there's space at the top for you to name the month with five weeks going across, and a little introduction before we go into the numbers. I know that not everybody gets paid a fixed amount at the beginning or end of every month, and that not every bill goes out on the first of the month, either, so my template gives you good visibility of what's coming in and going out, and when.

'Try to make a habit of planning your budget for each month at the end of the previous month, so that you feel prepared – and remember to check in on a weekly basis.'

Example month: *Name of month goes here*

INCOME

Source	Week 1	Week 2	Week 3	Week 4	Week 5

Total income:

Where the money comes from goes here, i.e. 'Clare Salary' or 'Child Benefit'

Even if the income is a monthly salary, place it in the week that corresponds with when it is paid - so if you get paid at the start of the month, place it in week 1

OUTGOINGS

Fixed outgoings	Week 1	Week 2	Week 3	Week 4	Week 5

Things like mortgage or rent and utilities go here

Total fixed outgoings: ....

Variable outgoings	Week 1	Week 2	Week 3	Week 4	Week 5

Things like petrol and food shopping go here – remember to use actual amounts rather than estimates

Total variable outgoings: ....

OUTGOINGS

Additional spending	Week 1	Week 2	Week 3	Week 4	Week 5
Any incidental spending goes here, whether planned or not					

Total additional spending: ....

DEBT REPAYMENTS

Debt	Week 1	Week 2	Week 3	Week 4	Week 5
List your debts and repayments here					

Total fixed outgoings: ....

THE BOTTOM LINE

Total money in	←— The total of all your income here
Total money out	←— The total of all your expenditure here
Total money saved	←— How much you've managed to save here
Money remaining	←— How much you're carrying over here

Now that you know how much disposable income you have, you can decide how you want to use it. Where is that money going?

Use this space to plan how you would like to use your disposable income every month

Month one: ....

So, here you are, poised at the starting line of a new way of running your finances. You might be nervous, or excited, or a little bit of both. Write down how you're feeling here:

....

Remember that this first month is about learning. It's not about getting it perfect right away, so let go of that inner perfectionist and allow yourself to be open to this process.

INCOME

Source	Week 1	Week 2	Week 3	Week 4	Week 5

Total income: ....

OUTGOINGS

Fixed outgoings	Week 1	Week 2	Week 3	Week 4	Week 5

Total fixed outgoings: ....

Variable outgoings	Week 1	Week 2	Week 3	Week 4	Week 5

Total variable outgoings: ....

OUTGOINGS

Additional spending	Week 1	Week 2	Week 3	Week 4	Week 5

Total additional spending: ....

DEBT REPAYMENTS

Debt	Week 1	Week 2	Week 3	Week 4	Week 5

Total fixed outgoings: ....

THE BOTTOM LINE

Total money in	
Total money out	
Total money saved	
Money remaining	

Now that you know how much disposable income you have, you can decide how you want to use it. Where is that money going?

....

....

....

....

....

....

....

....

....

....

Reflections at the end of your first month

Completing your first month of this new way of managing your money can throw up a whole load of mixed emotions – you might feel proud, disappointed or anywhere in between. Use the space below to write down how you're feeling now:

....

....

....

....

....

....

....

....

....

....

....

....

....

....

What have you learned?

I found that in the very early days of living with my budget, my eyes were opened to new observations about myself and my behaviour on an almost daily basis. Is there anything you've learned this month that you can use to build on your progress next month?

....

....

....

....

....

....

....

....

....

....

....

....

Month two: ....

You've got your first month under your belt now, and might be a little more confident going into this next budget. How are you feeling about the coming month?

....

Remember that this is about steady progress, so don't feel tempted to ramp things up too quickly if you overachieved last month – and don't feel too disheartened if you found it more difficult than you were anticipating.

INCOME

Source	Week 1	Week 2	Week 3	Week 4	Week 5

Total income: ....

OUTGOINGS

Fixed outgoings	Week 1	Week 2	Week 3	Week 4	Week 5

Total fixed outgoings: ....

Variable outgoings	Week 1	Week 2	Week 3	Week 4	Week 5

Total variable outgoings: ....

OUTGOINGS

Additional spending	Week 1	Week 2	Week 3	Week 4	Week 5

Total additional spending:..

DEBT REPAYMENTS

Debt	Week 1	Week 2	Week 3	Week 4	Week 5

Total fixed outgoings:......................................

THE BOTTOM LINE

Total money in	
Total money out	
Total money saved	
Money remaining	

Where is your disposable income being channelled this month?

....

....

....

....

....

....

....

....

....

....

....

Reflections at the end of your second month

By the end of this month, you may feel that you're getting the hang of things a little more, and you might even be able to see the start of some progress being made, both in your mindset and in your finances. Things might be happening a little more slowly, and that's fine, too. Make sure you take the space to decipher those emotions below:

....

....

....

....

....

....

....

....

....

....

....

....

....

Beating self-sabotage

As counter-intuitive as it might sound, I've noticed that human beings, and women in particular, sometimes feel the urge to ruin all of our progress the second we suspect that things are going too well. This could be down to complacency, which is something we need to watch out for, but it can also arise due to the fact that we don't always feel that we're worthy of success. Sometimes that shame monster that's been lurking in many of our wallets works in underhand ways – it sneaks into our consciousness and makes us question whether we're actually capable of maintaining positive changes in our lives, and whether we even deserve to feel happy and optimistic. We're so used to an internal narrative that tells us we are 'bad with money' that beginning to succeed with our finances feels alien to us – we feel like imposters in this new world.

It's often after a second month of success that these feelings start to creep in. We realise that it's not a fluke, but we still don't trust ourselves to keep it up – so now is a good time to address it. Have you been feeling the urge to self-sabotage? Write about how it's felt, and why you think those urges might be bubbling up:

....

....

....

....

It might help to flip back to your affirmations (page 63) and repeat them in a clear and convinced voice every time those negative voices get too loud.

Month three: ....

By month three, you've probably grown in confidence and learned a lot about yourself. You might have started to notice new habits beginning to feel more natural, and you may have begun to enjoy this process. Write about how you feel going into this new month:

....

This is the final month of budget-planning in this journal, but it definitely shouldn't be the end of your budgeting days. You can easily copy the format of these pages into a notebook or on to a spreadsheet, and continue in that way.

INCOME

Source	Week 1	Week 2	Week 3	Week 4	Week 5

Total income: ....

OUTGOINGS

Fixed outgoings	Week 1	Week 2	Week 3	Week 4	Week 5

Total fixed outgoings: ....

Variable outgoings	Week 1	Week 2	Week 3	Week 4	Week 5

Total variable outgoings: ....

OUTGOINGS

Additional spending	Week 1	Week 2	Week 3	Week 4	Week 5

Total additional spending: ....

DEBT REPAYMENTS

Debt	Week 1	Week 2	Week 3	Week 4	Week 5

Total fixed outgoings: ....

THE BOTTOM LINE

Total money in	
Total money out	
Total money saved	
Money remaining	

Where is your disposable income going this month?

....

....

....

....

....

....

....

....

....

....

....

Reflections at the end of your third month

By the time you're three months in, you should have started to notice a change in how you're feeling and how you're managing your money. Hopefully, you've started to detach your emotions from your spending habits and develop new ways of coping. You can reflect on the last three months here:

....

....

....

....

....

Dealing with budget fatigue

In some ways, the start is the easy part – it's keeping it up that's the challenge. For a couple of months, living with a budget can feel like a fun project, but life has a habit of getting in the way of the things we try to focus on, and it can be tiring. Some new habits might feel like second nature, while others might still feel like a bit of a drag. By this point, you may be feeling a little 'are we there yet?' about the whole thing, which is a sentiment that I'm very familiar with.

Try to remind yourself of the reasons you committed to this in the first place, and go back to those goals and progress-tracking tools earlier in the journal. Another thing that might help you to stay on track is looking through your budget and seeing if there's anywhere you can afford to allow yourself a little more breathing space, especially if there's something specific that you feel you're missing out on. If not, though, just make it all about those goals. It'll be worth it, I promise. In fact, now is a good moment to remind yourself of exactly why it's all going to be worth it. Write it here:

....

....

....

....

Your weekly plans

Having a monthly budget is great, but we all know that a week is more than just a small square on a single side of paper. Weeks contain a whole seven days' worth of life 'stuff' – and it's this 'stuff' that can make following the planned path that we've carefully laid out for ourselves feel difficult, if not impossible. For that reason, this journal also has these weekly pages in which you can track your expenses, mindset changes, progress, slip-ups, and basically everything that happens in between the monthly budgets.

On page 162, I talked about creating a weekly ritual, whereby you check in on your progress as part of a more general self-care routine. You can use the following pages to lend some structure to that session each week. This is a way of keeping yourself honest and accountable, but also makes sure that your needs aren't getting lost in your financial mission.

This section is intended to correspond roughly with your monthly budgets from the previous section, so you can use these weekly pages to track your progress as you work through the monthly budgets.

Week one

At this stage, you're probably still feeling quite raw and sensitive about things. You might feel a bit nervous and/or excited as you embark on this journey, and you might have found your first week tough or exhilarating. Write a little bit about how this week has gone here:

....

....

....

....

....

....

Is there something that's gone particularly well for you – something that you're proud of?

....

And have there been any slip-ups or sticky moments?

....

How has your spending been? Have there been any emotional or impulse purchases? If so, track them here, and don't forget to add them to your main monthly budget.

Purchase	Cost	Reasons

Have you progressed with any goals or hit any targets this week?

....

....

What are you aiming for or looking forward to next week?

....

....

Week two

You've had a week to settle into your new habits and to test out your new boundaries. You might be feeling a little restricted or frustrated, or that new-project motivation might be coursing through your veins. Write a little bit about how this week has gone here:

....

....

....

....

....

....

Is there something that's gone particularly well for you – something that you're proud of?

....

And have there been any slip-ups or sticky moments?

....

How has your spending been? Have there been any emotional or impulse purchases? If so, track them here, and don't forget to add them to your main monthly budget.

Purchase	Cost	Reasons

Have you progressed with any goals or hit any targets this week?

....

....

What are you aiming for or looking forward to next week?

....

....

Week three

The third week of the month can be a tricky one, as it's often when it starts to feel like the money is running out. Checking your bank balance this week, you might feel pleasantly surprised at how your new habits are affecting your available funds – or you might still feel wary. Write a little bit about how this week has gone here:

....

....

....

....

....

....

Is there something that's gone particularly well for you – something that you're proud of?

....

And have there been any slip-ups or sticky moments?

....

How has your spending been? Have there been any emotional or impulse purchases? If so, track them here, and don't forget to add them to your main monthly budget.

Purchase	Cost	Reasons

Have you progressed with any goals or hit any targets this week?

....

....

What are you aiming for or looking forward to next week?

....

....

Week four

You're coming to the end of your first month of this part of the journal, and you might have noticed a difference in how you're feeling now compared to how you usually feel towards the end of the month. Hopefully you feel a little more in control and a little less anxious, but these are still very early days, and it's fine if you're not. Write a little bit about how this week has gone here:

....

....

....

....

....

....

Is there something that's gone particularly well for you – something that you're proud of?

....

And have there been any slip-ups or sticky moments?

....

How has your spending been? Have there been any emotional or impulse purchases? If so, track them here, and don't forget to add them to your main monthly budget.

Purchase	Cost	Reasons

Have you progressed with any goals or hit any targets this week?

....

....

What are you aiming for or looking forward to next week?

....

....

Week five

A new month beckons. Trying not to slip into old habits on payday can be hard once the initial rush of gaining control has subsided, but try to remember why you started this. Write a little bit about how this week has gone here:

....

....

....

....

....

....

Is there something that's gone particularly well for you – something that you're proud of?

....

And have there been any slip-ups or sticky moments?

....

How has your spending been? Have there been any emotional or impulse purchases? If so, track them here, and don't forget to add them to your main monthly budget.

Purchase	Cost	Reasons

Have you progressed with any goals or hit any targets this week?

....

....

What are you aiming for or looking forward to next week?

....

....

Week six

You may find that your new habits are starting to feeling a bit more automatic now, or you might find that new challenges are arising. Write a little bit about how this week has gone here:

....

....

....

....

....

....

Is there something that's gone particularly well for you – something that you're proud of?

....

And have there been any slip-ups or sticky moments?

....

How has your spending been? Have there been any emotional or impulse purchases? If so, track them here, and don't forget to add them to your main monthly budget.

Purchase	Cost	Reasons

Have you progressed with any goals or hit any targets this week?

....

....

What are you aiming for or looking forward to next week?

....

....

Week seven

Think about how you feel about things now compared to this time last month, and the month before. How have things changed? Write a little bit about how this week has gone here:

....

....

....

....

....

....

Is there something that's gone particularly well for you – something that you're proud of?

....

And have there been any slip-ups or sticky moments?

....

How has your spending been? Have there been any emotional or impulse purchases? If so, track them here, and don't forget to add them to your main monthly budget.

Purchase	Cost	Reasons

Have you progressed with any goals or hit any targets this week?

....

....

What are you aiming for or looking forward to next week?

....

....

Week eight

As you approach the two-month mark, you might have started to see a few material changes in your circumstances. Write a little bit about how this week has gone here:

....

....

....

....

....

....

Is there something that's gone particularly well for you – something that you're proud of?

....

And have there been any slip-ups or sticky moments?

....

How has your spending been? Have there been any emotional or impulse purchases? If so, track them here, and don't forget to add them to your main monthly budget.

Purchase	Cost	Reasons

Have you progressed with any goals or hit any targets this week?

....

....

What are you aiming for or looking forward to next week?

....

....

Week nine

Have you noticed a change in your behaviour around the end of the month and payday? Does the cycle feel a little more evenly spaced? Do things feel more balanced? Write a little bit about how this week has gone here:

....

....

....

....

....

....

Is there something that's gone particularly well for you – something that you're proud of?

....

And have there been any slip-ups or sticky moments?

....

How has your spending been? Have there been any emotional or impulse purchases? If so, track them here, and don't forget to add them to your main monthly budget.

Purchase	Cost	Reasons

Have you progressed with any goals or hit any targets this week?

....

....

What are you aiming for or looking forward to next week?

....

....

Week ten

You might be starting to feel a little fatigued at this point, now that the initial buzz has well and truly worn off. Think about what it is that's motivating you to continue now. Write a little bit about how this week has gone here:

....

....

....

....

....

....

Is there something that's gone particularly well for you – something that you're proud of?

....

And have there been any slip-ups or sticky moments?

....

How has your spending been? Have there been any emotional or impulse purchases? If so, track them here, and don't forget to add them to your main monthly budget.

Purchase	Cost	Reasons

Have you progressed with any goals or hit any targets this week?

....

....

What are you aiming for or looking forward to next week?

....

....

Week eleven

Things might be starting to feel a little more balanced now, in terms of both your finances and your emotions. Make sure you're reinforcing positive behaviour and trying to understand any setbacks as you continue forwards. Write a little bit about how this week has gone here:

....

....

....

....

....

....

Is there something that's gone particularly well for you – something that you're proud of?

....

And have there been any slip-ups or sticky moments?

....

How has your spending been? Have there been any emotional or impulse purchases? If so, track them here, and don't forget to add them to your main monthly budget.

Purchase	Cost	Reasons

Have you progressed with any goals or hit any targets this week?

....

....

What are you aiming for or looking forward to next week?

....

....

Week twelve

This week is the last structured week in this journal, so it's a good idea to think about how you're going to continue this consciousness around money going forward. The idea might make you feel a bit nervous, or you might feel ready and raring to go. Write a little bit about how this week has gone, and how you feel about carrying on here:

....

....

....

....

....

....

Is there something that's gone particularly well for you – something that you're proud of?

....

And have there been any slip-ups or sticky moments?

....

How has your spending been? Have there been any emotional or impulse purchases? If so, track them here, and don't forget to add them to your main monthly budget.

Purchase	Cost	Reasons

Have you progressed with any goals or hit any targets this week?

....

....

What are you aiming for or looking forward to next week?

....

....

You did it!

This section is the most long-lasting and labour-intensive, so take a moment to congratulate yourself if you've come to the end of it! You're very close to completing the journal, and I really hope that life is looking quite different for you now. There's space to reflect on this in the next, final section.

Chapter Nine
Reflections

The beauty of this journal is that it will fall into everyone's hands in exactly the same state – crisp, pristine and ready to be filled in – but by the time you reach this last section, your book will be completely unique to you. It will be filled with achievements, challenges and disappointments, and it will hopefully have charted your journey as you improve both your relationship with money and your financial situation. There will be notes in the margins, crossings out, goals achieved and progress made.

Now is the time to reflect on the last few months, or however long it's taken you to get to this point. What have you learned about yourself? What's changed? Take a few minutes to write about your achievements, targets you've reached, and possibly the setbacks you've dealt with, too:

....

....

....

....

....

....

....

....

....

Look back at the vision that you drew in the goals section. Has it changed at all? You're probably not 'there' yet, but does it feel closer now? If there's a difference between the vision you drew then and the one you envisage now, use this space to draw out your new vision with words and doodles.

As I mentioned previously, progress is very rarely linear. It's likely that you've experienced both triumphs and disappointments so far, which is entirely normal. Can you pinpoint a few setbacks, and write about what they have taught you?

....

....

....

....

....

....

....

Changing habits, coping mechanisms and attitudes

It's likely that, in order to succeed, you've developed new, more positive habits and coping mechanisms. Opinions on how long it takes to form a habit vary, but the general consensus is that it's somewhere between 18 and 254 days, with an average of 66 days, depending on the behaviour it is that you're trying to change. The same study strongly recommends replacing an old habit with a new one in order to overcome negative behaviour, because it's very difficult to simply break a habit and leave a vacuum in its place. Take some time to think about your new habits, and how they compare to your old habits.

Old habit/coping mechanism/ attitude	New habit/coping mechanism/ attitude

Take a little bit of time to really appreciate these changes, thinking about what they've done for you so far and what they'll do for you in the future. This is big, life-changing stuff, and I want you to feel the full weight of what you've achieved.

Your financial wellbeing now

In addition to all of the things that are quite difficult to measure, like how you feel and the state of your mental health, there may also be some more measurable outcomes of the changes you've made since starting this journal. Look back at the numbers you wrote down in the very first section of this journal, on page 22. How do you feel looking at those starting figures now?

....

....

....

Now, look at the same measures for your current financial situation.

Current account balance (s)

....

Current total debt

....

Current total savings/investments/assets

....

....

Can you see progress? Is there a reduction in your debt or an increase in your savings or assets?

Change in current account balance(s)

....

Change in total debt

....

Change in total savings/investments/assets

....

....

How do you feel when you look at the progress you've made? Does it just feel good, or are there some more complex feelings at play?

....

....

....

....

....

....

....

....

....

Has the way that you think and feel about money changed since the start of this journal? Think about situations that used to leave you feeling anxious, or the ways in which you have responded to feeling low or depressed in the past. Are there any differences now?

....

....

....

....

....

....

....

....

....

....

....

....

....

....

Continuing the good work

Of course, it's not likely that this is goodbye forever. Hopefully your work with this journal will continue long after you read this final page. Hopefully you'll continue to revisit and revamp your goals, and return again and again to colour in your squares and battle on and on until you reach those much-desired and hard fought-for targets. For many of us, the process of cultivating a healthier and more positive relationship with money is a lengthy one, and not necessarily one that's always completely within our control, so it would make me incredibly happy if you were to keep this journal as a demonstration of what you can achieve when you set your mind to it.

I hope that you'll come back to this book if and when you feel old habits and behaviours start to creep back in, but mainly I hope that you'll use it as a jumping-off point to keep making improvements to both your relationship with money and your financial situation.

Have a think about what's next for you now, and how you can continue the work that you've done here.

....

....

....

....

....

If you've found it helpful, I hope that you'll continue to journal as a way to organise your finances and process the feelings that go along with them. It's a brilliant way to spot patterns and understand behaviour, in life as well as in money. Good luck!

Further reading/watching/listening

On guilt and shame
- Brené Brown's TED Talks (ted.com/speakers/brene_brown)
- Anxiety UK (www.anxietycare.org.uk/anxiety/guilt-and-shame)
- Beverly Engel's article on self-forgiveness for *Psychology Today* (www.psychologytoday.com/gb/blog/the-compassion-chronicles/201706/healing-your-shame-and-guilt-through-self-forgiveness)

On mental health
- Andrew Solomon's TED Talks (ted.com/speakers/andrew_solomon)
- *A Toolkit for Modern Life: 53 Ways to Look After Your Mind* by Dr Emma Hepburn
- *Feel Better, Live More* podcast with Dr Rangan Chatterjee

On money management
Websites
- The Money Advice Service (www.moneyadviceservice.org.uk)
- Vestpod (www.vestpod.com)
- Money Saving Expert (www.moneysavingexpert.com)

Books
- *Money: A User's Guide* by Laura Whateley
- *Open Up* by Alex Holder
- *Go Fund Yourself* by Alice Tapper
- *You're Not Broke, You're Pre-Rich* by Emilie Bellet
- *Real Life Money* by Clare Seal (that's me!)

Instagram accounts
- @moneymedics
- @vestpod
- @go_fund_yourself
- @mrmoneyjar
- @thebudgetnista
- @myfrugalyear (me again!)

Notes

Acknowledgements

Writing a book during a pandemic is not an easy task, and I couldn't have done it without the support of those close to me. My husband, Phil, helped me not to doubt myself when I was having the most horrible bout of imposter syndrome. My mum whisked me away for a weekend in the countryside so that I could get some headspace (and some extra help with my children). My sisters and friends were always at the end of a phone call or WhatsApp message, and my Instagram community were a huge support. I'm also so grateful for the valuable contributions from Emilie and Zoe.

I'd also really love to thank my agent, Julia, for her words of support and enthusiasm, and Anna, Kate, Jessica and the whole Headline team for helping me to make this journal happen.

Lastly, I'd really like to thank you, the reader, for committing yourself to this journal, and to changing your relationship with money.